Practical Bicycle Buyers Guide

Peter Eland

Edited by Richard Ballantine

snowbooks
LONDON

Proudly published in the UK, in 2009, by:
Snowbooks Ltd.
120 Pentonville Road
London
N1 9JN
email: info@snowbooks.com
www.snowbooks.com

British Library Cataloguing in Publication Data
A catalogue record for this book is available from the British Library.
ISBN 13 978-1-905005-857

Picture credits:

Sue Holden: p. 118, p. 124 bottom, p. 125 top Jason Patient: p. 124 top Dave Mountain: p. 131
Richard Ballantine p.160 and hack bike p. 73

Product studio and promotional images are by the various manufacturers as identified in
the accompanying text.

All other images by Peter Eland.

Printed and bound in Great Britain

Contents

Introduction

Ever more people are discovering cycling – perhaps as an efficient way to get to work, or perhaps just as a leisure activity for summer weekends. With a good bike and good advice the experience should be a positive one.

And once you're cycling, the elegant minimalism of pedalling as a form of transport becomes apparent. It's fun, it's quiet, it's reliable, it's cheap, it's invigorating. It's environmental and it's community-friendly. It's simply a more pleasant experience – physically and psychologically – than any other form of travel.

So why not do more by bike? Few realise the sheer diversity of cycling techniques and technology which exist to enable you to fulfil a wide range of transport tasks by pedal power, safely and enjoyably.

From moving a washing machine to transporting a gaggle of children to school, there are bikes that can do it. If you need to take a bike on the train, bus or taxi to reach a distant destination door-to-door, then a folding bike exists for every budget. Bikes and adaptations for injured or disabled riders provide real independent mobility. And touring bikes and recumbents offer comfortable, mile-eating cycling for anything from a day-ride to a trans-continental adventure.

If there's a single theme which links all of the bikes described in this book, it's the use of cycling as a practical form of transport. So you won't find racing bikes, mountain bikes or any competitive cycling in these pages.

What you will find is a selection of the techniques and equipment which have enabled me, a non-driver, to complete my day-to-day journeys and tasks safely and enjoyably over two decades. The book also draws upon the experiences of many friends and contributors to *Velo Vision*, the quarterly magazine of practical cycling and innovative cycle design which I publish. See *www.velovision.com* or phone 01904 438 224 for details, for a sample or to subscribe. Much of the material has been updated from 'Buyer's Guides' published in the magazine over the last few years.

'Buyer's Guide' implies a quick overview which the reader can skim for 'Recommended' and 'Best Buy' labels. But a bike is something to which you trust your life in traffic, and its purchase deserves some in-depth investigation. So before getting down to the nitty-gritty of things you can actually buy, I'll start with a first-principles look at the most basic of bicycle systems, braking and gearing. Understanding these key systems will inform any bicycle purchase and make it more likely to fulfil your cycling needs. Then we'll look at some other important elements of the bike which, when you get them right, can hugely enhance the riding experience.

After that we'll start the Buyer's Guide itself with town bikes – my take on the city cycling at the core of most transport cyclists' experience. We'll then look at folding bikes, family cycling, special needs cycling and load-carrying by bike, before heading off to touring bikes and recumbents, the comfortable way to ride all day.

Along the way I hope you'll be delighted by the diversity, amazed at the engineering, and impressed by the ingenuity of some of the designs we present, designed and developed by a worldwide community of manufacturers passionate about practical cycling. And I hope you'll be inspired and empowered to do even more by bike.

Peter Eland

Bicycling basics

Gearing: it drives your bike

"How many gears has it got, mister?" is a stock question from kids admiring a fine bike. Rightly or wrongly, number of gears seems to have become a metric of a bike's quality – in the public mind at least. 24 has to be better than 21, right? And who would choose to ride a lowly three-speed these days?

Yet it's hard to think of a less meaningful question to ask about gears. 'How many' is a handy marketing tool, but the answer has almost nothing to do with how useful those gears will be to you as a cyclist.

So in this section we'll focus on the basics of gearing.

Why are they necessary? What do gears actually do? And how should you go about choosing a system which will fit your needs as a cyclist – and your budget?

Why use gears?

The starting point for any discussion about cycle technology should be, but often isn't, the human body. So it is with gearing.

The human body wasn't designed to ride a bicycle. The legs evolved primarily for walking, running and swimming. That gave them a certain action and strength, and a certain speed range at which they can operate comfortably. That would typically be from a step a second or thereabouts for a slow walk, to several times that at a run. Kicking as you swim is in between.

Put that same body over a pair of pedals and the legs still favour the same sort of rhythm or cadence. A pace a second equates to 60 turns a minute or so. Experience shows that most people prefer to pedal at a rate somewhere between say 50 to 150 rotations per minute (rpm). But the 'comfort zone' within that range will be much smaller for each particular cyclist. I know that I like pedalling around 90 rpm, and even dropping to 70 starts to feel less than ideal.

Beginning cyclists tend to prefer to pedal slower, around the 60 rpm mark or less, while more experienced cyclists prefer pedalling faster (known as a 'higher cadence'), probably because this means less straining on the knee in the longer term.

But in any case, the human body only likes to have its pedalling speed varied within a small range, say plus or minus 15-20% of whatever speed is 'ideal'. Now a bicycle's speed clearly varies by much more than that: from zero (at a standstill) to bowling along with a tailwind or downhill. Gears are simply a way to allow you to keep pedalling at your preferred rate, while the speed of the cycle varies.

Even on a single-speed bike you have gearing: it's just set at a single ratio which will put you into your preferred rate-of-pedalling range when you're riding along at 'normal' speed. When you're starting off, or going up a hill, you'll be pedalling slower than is comfortable, straining at the pedals, possibly rising out of the saddle to apply more force. And as your speed rises, downhill for example, your feet will end up twiddling as fast as you can move them.

What variable gearing ('lots of gears') does is let you change the ratio, allowing you to pedal comfortably and efficiently while the bike changes speed. If you hit a hill, instead of straining you can change to a lower gear. This just means that for each turn of your pedals, the rear wheel turns rather fewer times than before, so you go slower. In a tailwind, you can shift to a higher gear, meaning that you can continue to add to the speed of the bike by pedalling without having to lash your legs up and down uncomfortably fast.

There are many and varied ways of achieving variable gearing. Some cover a wider range of speeds than others. So what's really necessary?

Ratio range required

It's tempting to imagine two extremes of speed: at the slow end might be grinding up a steep slope into a headwind with full camping gear, on a tricycle, at a speed of perhaps 2 km/h. At the other end might be descending a long mountain pass with a following wind at perhaps 60 km/h. Divide the one by the other and you get a 30:1 or 3000% ratio. In other words, if a gearing system were to let you pedal at a constant rate through that whole range of speeds, the top gear would need to take you 30 times further per turn of the pedals than the lowest.

Unfortunately nobody has yet invented a practical gearing system which will do this, so compromise is necessary – often lots of compromise. Thankfully the human body is rather adaptable, and can do quite well with the much smaller ranges, at best around 7:1, which turn out to be mechanically practical. And of course most riders won't be pedalling in anything like such extreme circumstances.

Experience shows that the following ranges are generally preferred as a minimum by most utility and touring riders. Strong riders can often get away with reduced gear range. Overleaf are shown the typical systems which achieve these ranges. Unfortunately as the range increases, so generally does the weight, cost and maintenance.

FLAT URBAN UTILITY CYCLING:

» 2:1 (also known as 200%)

» About the range of most three-speed hub gears. Some riders get by with a single speed.

SPORTY FLAT URBAN CYCLING, OR SOME HILLS:

» 3:1 or 300% or more

» Seven, eight or nine-speed hub gears, or single-chainring derailleur systems.

ANYTHING REALLY HILLY OR MORE DEMANDING:

» 5:1 or 500% or more

» Triple-ring derailleur system, combined hub/derailleur systems or the Rohloff hub gear

SPECIAL APPLICATIONS:

» 7:1 or 700% or more

» Combined or multiple hub and derailleur systems for touring tandems, recumbent trikes and anyone who likes a really wide range!

Hubs and derailleurs

There are two main types of gearing systems: hub and derailleur.

A hub gear system has its mechanism contained within the shell of the rear hub, and it's usually driven by a wide, robust chain running from a single chainring at the front to a single cog at the back, as in the picture to the right.

A derailleur system employs multiple cogs on the back wheel and often several front chainrings, and it is the different sizes of these which set the ratio. The thin flexible chain is guided by shifting mechanisms called 'derailleurs', a French word roughly meaning 'de-railers' (think trains). They simply shove the chain sideways off one sprocket so that (if all goes well) it falls neatly onto the next. The inventor is said to have remarked "*C'est brutal, mais ca marche,*" (It's crude, but it works)!

So how many speeds?

The full range of any gearing system is actually achieved by having a number of set speeds: particular ratios spread (ideally) evenly across the range, between which you can shift as your bike speed changes. You'll generally have little choice if using commercial systems, but jumps of around 15% or so are usually considered sufficiently finely spaced. Any jump over 25% or so feels a bit 'wide', jarring to the legs which suddenly have to make a big jump in pedalling speed. Almost all of the commercial systems stick within these limits.

How gears are measured

Gear ranges are sometimes mentioned in bike reviews, and can usually be worked out from the manufacturer's specification if not. It's worth knowing what the figures mean.

A touring bike, for example, might have a range of 21" to 104". Those measurements are in 'gear inches', most easily visualised as the diameter of penny-farthing wheel which would go the same distance per turn of the pedals. But most cyclists just go by experience: anything below 30 is a low touring gear, and anything over 100 is a tailwinds-only overdrive.

Practical cyclists will choose a range to match their riding. If you commute over flat terrain, 40-90" will normally be plenty. Tow heavy trailers, or add some hills, and you'd prefer a low of 30" or less. The same applies to carrying children in child seats or pulling child trailers – the extra weight means you'll need the lower gears.

At this point I could go into the maths of it all, but I don't really have space and I'd rather write about something more interesting. If you're keen to learn more look up bicycle gear ratios on the internet, for example at Sheldon Brown's website: *www.sheldonbrown.com.*

Other considerations

While the overall gear range you need for your particular type of cycling is a good starting point, your final choice of gearing system will no doubt be influenced by many more factors, often conflicting. Among them may be:

» *Cost:* You can get a very wide-range derailleur system much more cheaply than the equivalent hub gear. But the hub gear should last longer, and cheap derailleurs aren't nice to work with.

» *Weight:* this tends to reduce as price increases. Derailleur systems tend to be lighter than hub gears.

» *Efficiency:* A certain amount of the energy you put into the pedals will always be lost to friction in the gearing mechanism. A well-oiled chain is remarkably efficient: up to 98%+, but chain efficiency does fall with rust and with lack of lubrication. There are also noticeable friction losses when a chain is wrapped around a small sprocket, so in general larger sprockets are easier-running (but heavier). Hub gears usually have a chain drive first, then a complex gear mechanism inside the hub, so two chances to lose efficiency. In practice, the difference may be less clear-cut, especially if you're like me and feel that life is too short to waste cleaning oily bike chains. A hub gear system can easily be as efficient as a grimy derailleur set-up and takes much less maintenance. My recommendation is hub gears for everyday use, and a derailleur bike for weekend or faster riding.

» *Shifting skill required:* Some hub gears, such as the Shimano 7-speeds, are nearly impossible to damage by clumsy shifting. You can change gear while moving, while stopped or while pedalling under load. You can back-pedal whenever you like. That's not the case with all hub gears, and it's certainly not the case with derailleurs. While Shimano and others have made major improvements in ease of use, derailleur gears do require a bit more skill and care. The combination of front and rear changers is also confusing to many: hub gears just tend to have a single twist grip to take you through the whole range.

» *Maintenance:* As a general rule hub gears are very low maintenance, and can soldier on for years with hardly a moment's attention. But if they do break down there's not a lot you can do to fix them yourself.

Derailleur systems require more attention, chain cleaning and adjustment in daily use, but everything is out in the open and if something does go wrong it can be fixed more or less anywhere in the world.

» *Frame fit:* Some transmission systems require a frame built for the purpose. Hub gears can often be fitted into a frame originally designed for derailleurs, for example, but some fiddling may be required.

» *Wheel size:* Most transmission systems are designed for bikes with full-sized wheels (26" to 28"), so when they're used on small-wheeled bikes the gearing will often be lower than intended by the designer. The usual way to compensate for this is to use a huge front chainring. But as really low gears are useful and can often otherwise be tricky to achieve, many riders see this lowering as a bonus.

» *Brake compatibility:* If you want a rear disk brake, only a few hub gears offer appropriate mounts – but there are disk brake hubs for all derailleur systems.

» *Shifter types:* You may prefer a particular type of gear shifter, or require it to fit your handlebar setup. There's usually a choice between a twistgrip type and a 'button' or lever type shifter for most systems, although some hub gears are more restricted.

Twist grip changers are popular for folding bikes, as they're robust and unlikely to be knocked out of position when folding. They're less ideal on some bikes where the twisting action can inadvertently affect the steering – bar end or trigger/button shifters may be better.

Hub gears

Hub gears really are tremendous gears for the non-technical cyclist: once they're fitted, chances are they'll work trouble-free for years. Today's hub gears have more to offer than ever before, with new models offering plenty of gears, wide range, slick shifting and stylish design.

Hub gears do sometimes suffer on the shop floor: they aren't as glamorous as derailleur-geared bikes which are more shiny, have racing heritage, and keep the dealer's repair department busier! So you may not find much choice of hub gear bikes in stock at your local bike shop. But if you're looking for reliable town transport, do make the effort to seek hub gears out.

Hub gear strengths

» Low maintenance! Hub gears can go for literally years before requiring attention. All the delicate internals are sealed away inside, either in an oil bath or 'sealed for life' in grease.

» No real need to clean the chain! Of course a clean chain is good, and will be smoother and last longer, but unlike a derailleur system, a hub gear will work just as well however caked in gunk your chain may be.

» An even better solution which is relatively easy with hub gears is to fit a chaincase, which encloses the chain entirely, keeping both it and your trousers clean. This isn't possible for derailleur gears.

» The wide chains used on hub gear systems last much longer than the narrow, delicate ones used on derailleur system. They're usually cheaper, too! Wider chains are also less flexible, so hardly ever 'fall off' chainring or sprockets unintentionally.

» Hub gears usually means stronger wheels. Because there's no need to squeeze in 8 or 9 sprockets on one side, the hub can be much more symmetrical, making for more even spoke tension from side to side.

» You can change gear at any time – either at a standstill or while pedalling. Some modern hubs let you shift under load, too.

» Hub gears are robust and less easily damaged by unskilled riders or a chance knock than derailleur gears.

Hub gear weaknesses

» Weight: most hub gear systems weigh more than a derailleur set-up of comparable range. The weight is also concentrated at the back wheel, which may be particularly unfavourable for bikes with suspension.

» Efficiency: all those little gears meshing together, plus the chain drive too, mean that hub gears do have more losses than a clean derailleur drive. But the difference narrows as the derailleur chain gets dirty, and for most hub gears any speed difference may not be noticeable for most riders. Some hubs do have certain gears which feel noticeably 'like treacle' but then again, some derailleur gears aren't that good either, as we'll see in the next chapter.

» Emergency repair: if a hub gear does break when you're on the road there's not usually much you can do, whereas derailleur gears can often be temporarily fixed.

» Bulk: the larger hub shells of hub gears can make for extreme spoke angles in very small wheels – occasionally a problem for recumbents and folders.

» Cost: there are a lot of highly-stressed, precision-formed gears and other parts in a hub gear, and there is a limit to how cheaply these can be made. Cheaper derailleur system are certainly possible – but a hub gear should outlast them comfortably.

How do hub gears work?

Hub gears use a system of internal gears to make the wheel turn either faster or slower than the rear sprocket, which is driven by the chain from the front chainring. So there are two stages to the system: the chain drive to the rear cog, then the second system within the rear hub.

The range of the second part – within the hub gear – is set when you buy your chosen system. But the whole range can be shifted higher or lower by the choice of chainring and cog sizes, although there is a limit as to how low you can go.

Which hub gear?

The first step in choosing a hub gear is to determine the gear range you require – see the previous chapter. Price will tend to rise as gear range increases.

Then, within each of the ranges there are likely to be several competing hub gears – for example, if you're just after a three-speed, then there will be options from all three major manufacturers. At the wide-range end, there are 8-speeds from both Shimano and Sturmey, plus a 9-speed from SRAM.

If you're technically-minded, you could look up the exact ratios of the hubs in question, trawl the internet for feedback on reliability and efficiency, and make the 'perfect' decision. A more pragmatic approach might be to see which maker's hub your local dealer can get and repair, and stick to that.

There might also be limited choices if you prefer a certain type of brake: not all hubs have the relevant fixings for disk brakes, for example. Another factor to consider is whether there's a shift mechanism sticking out of the axle end, as with the SRAM 'Clickbox' (on most of their hubs except the 9-speed) or the similar Shimano Intego device. Most recent hubs tuck the shifting mechanism away inside the frame where it's less vulnerable (but perhaps less easy to disconnect).

Most hubs are available via dealers. Many models do seem to take some time to come available in the UK: often they're first seen fitted as original equipment on complete bikes. There's a listing of some specialist dealers at the end of this report who may be able to help. As an alternative, some customers buy over the internet from shops in the Netherlands or Germany, where the selection tends to be wider.

Shimano

Shimano offer hub gears in 3, 7 and 8-speed versions, plus the Intego (8-speed derailleur plus 3-speed hub gear,) and Alfine (8-speed hub gear with – optionally – two front chainrings) systems. Their hubs are known for excellent smooth shifting, even under load, but sometimes with less even jumps between gears, and in some gears less efficiency, than the competition. That said, few riders will be troubled by either of these niggles.

Most of the Shimano hubs are available with fittings for roller brakes, and come in coaster (backpedal brake) versions too. The new Alfine version of the 8-speed accepts disk brakes.

See www.shimano-eu.com for full technical details.

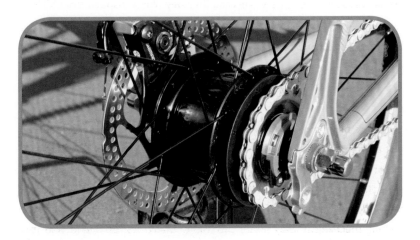

The Shimano Alpine 8-speed hub

SRAM

SRAM make 3, 5, 7 and 9-speed models, plus the DualDrive system (9-speed derailleur and three-speed hub gear). SRAM hubs are seen as efficient, wide-range and reliable. A program of modernisation of the old Sachs designs means that shifting is generally now much improved with lighter action, and rivals the Shimano models.

Most of the SRAM models come in coaster brake or i-Brake versions as well as plain hubs. The DualDrive and new 'i-Motion' 9-speed will fit disk brakes, too. See www.sram.com for full technical details.

Sunrace Sturmey-Archer

After its rebirth in Taiwan following the UK company's collapse a few years ago, Sturmey has rapidly returned to production and has also been bringing out new products at quite a pace. They have 3, 5 and 8-speed hubs currently, all in drum brake or plain versions (plus many more options for the three-speed), and the 8-speed now comes in a disk brake version too. After some teething troubles the 8-speed now appears to be approaching the reliability of the well-proven 3-speed design, and an updated version is expected for 2009.

See www.sturmey-archer.com for full details.

Rohloff

Standing alone with a super-wide range is the Rohloff 14-speed 'Speedhub', with even 13.6% gaps between its gears and an overall range of

The Rohloff Speedhub 14-speed.

526%. It's beautifully made and has a price-tag (£500+) to match. Users report that the hub just lasts and lasts. Some have mentioned that it's a little loud at first, but this does seem to quieten down after some use. A unique device to replace a full-range derailleur system.

There are several versions to fit different frame types, and a disk brake can be fitted. They're rated for tandem use, too.

See www.rohloff.de for full details.

Other hub-type gears

Schlumpf drives

Made in Switzerland for over a decade now, the Schlumpf Drive family is a wonderfully simple way to add gearing range to any existing set-up. A new bottom bracket and crankset replaces the existing parts on your bike, and built into the new set is a two-speed epicyclic gearbox, with the gears shifted via a tap of the heel on the axle end.

There are now three versions:

» *Mountain Drive:* this gives direct drive and a stump-pulling 2.5 times reduction – so if you have a 50-tooth chainring, in low gear it'll rotate only once for every 2.5 turns of the pedals, behaving like a 20-tooth ring. Good for adding touring gears to an otherwise sporty bike.

» *Speed Drive:* this gives direct drive and 1.65 times overdrive – so it's as if you have a bigger ring than you do. This can help with small-wheeled bikes, allowing good speeds without excessively large chainrings.

» *High Speed Drive:* this gives direct drive and a more extreme 2.5x times overdrive.

The drives may need to be installed by a dealer with a special chamfering tool (or it can be hired from e.g. Kinetics in the UK) but they really will fit on almost any bike. Special kits are available for Brompton, Birdy and Dahon

YOUR RECEIPT
THANK YOU
CALL AGAIN

JUST
BOOKS

REC   25-06-2018 01:34 PM
                      000026

1 BARGIN BOOKS   £0.50
  TOTAL   £0.50
  CASH   £0.50

folders. I've had a Mountain Drive on my own Birdy for many years now and it's never faltered, and I've even used the 9" bottom gear a few times! Most of the drives are now rated for use with tandem and even fixed gear bikes, but check with Schlumpf to be certain.

One real drawback to the Schlumpf drives is the cost: at around £250+ each in the UK, combining one with say an 8-speed hub gear setup starts to approach the price of a Rohloff hub. But for many applications they offer a superbly simple and neat wide gear range solution.

For 2009 SRAM have announced their 'Hammerschmidt' system, which operates similarly to the Schlumpf Speed Drive, but with gear changing via a handlebar-mounted shifter instead of the axle-end buttons. Two fairly high-end mountain bike versions are planned

initially, and reports suggest that prices will be comparable with (or even more than) for the Schlumpf models.

See www.schlumpf.ch or phone +41 81 723 8009 for full technical details.

NuVinci CVT

The 'NuVinci' continuously-variable drive promises a smoothly variable hub transmission, with 350% range. It's now available on a number of up-market town bikes, and it works very well. The lack of distinct gears makes it very easy to use: just twist the shifter one way for easier pedalling or the other way for more resistance. The drawbacks so far are weight (4 kg!) and to some extent cost, though the manufacturers say they expect to introduce a lighter version in due course. Efficiency is also a possible issue.

The ease of use, though, is the NuVinci's stand-out quality. It's practically impossible to damage by lack of skill in shifting, and these arguably overbuilt, heavy hubs have even higher torque ratings than the Rohloff. Perhaps they could be the perfect low-maintenance hub for heavy use on workbikes or hire centre machines.

Currently the hubs are available built into bikes from a number of US and mainland Europe manufacturers (see the website for a full list). In the UK, try www.amstelcycles.co.uk. The hub is also available separately, but currently only by ordering direct from the USA. See www.fallbrooktech.com for full technical details.

UK hub gear specialists

There are far more bike shops who know their way around hub gears than I can list here. Just about any dealer who offers utility cycles or continental-style hub-geared bikes will be familiar with everyday adjustments and minor fixes. And just about any dealer can order hub gears through the usual trade suppliers. So at the risk of offending all those who aren't mentioned, I've just

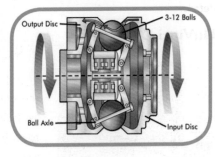

listed below a few contacts who are particular specialists:

» Bicycle Workshop: London SRAM and Sturmey repair and parts specialists. Tel 020 7229 4850 or see www.bicycleworkshop.co.uk

» Brixton Cycles: London dealers who do many hub gear bikes: 020 7733 6055 or see www.brixtoncycles.co.uk

» Cycle Heaven: York dealer specialising in hub gear bikes: Tel 01904 651870 or see www.cycleheaven.co.uk

» Kinetics: Glasgow specialists for Rohloff and Schlumpf drives: Tel 0141 942 2552 or see www.kinetics.org.uk

» Roman Road Cycles: SRAM and Sturmey hub gear specialists. Tel 01558 650336 or see www.roman-road.co.uk

» Tony Hadland's website: contains many hub gear resources, especially for Sturmey hubs, including much historical and repair information. See: www.hadland.net

» Phoenix Hub Gear Repairs: 01908 320868 or email firebird3101@yahoo.co.uk

» Old Bike Trader: Tel (0)20 8306 0060 or see www.oldbiketrader.co.uk

Derailleur gears

Derailleur gears are often the choice of racers, touring cyclists, off-road riders – and many more cycle users who just buy what's available at a good price. Overwhelmingly, in the UK at least, derailleurs dominate the cycling landscape from 'supermarket specials' at the lowest possible price-point to high-end racing bikes and MTBs at the 'silly money' end.

This is not without good reason. Derailleur gears are a simple solution to the gearing problem, a basic mechanism which can be made to work well at all levels of price and quality. They are easily repaired, with all of the workings on show, in plain sight.

They're also just more fun! The proof is in the riding: jumping onto a well-maintained derailleur bike can be a revelation after trundling around town on hub gears. There's effortless smoothness in every gear, while every hub I've tried has some gears rougher, or louder, than others. Often the gaps between gears are smaller and more evenly spaced, making it easier to keep on pedalling at your preferred cadence. And there's the shifting itself: on modern systems it's so good that you can hardly feel through the pedals as the chain snicks across the rear sprockets, even under quite some load. There's also a certain feeling of skill involved with derailleurs, and a satisfaction as you click through the gears, remembering to downshift before you stop or hit that hill…

The open nature of derailleur gearing is its weakness: it's very difficult to keep the chain and sprockets from getting covered in dirt. It's hard to guarantee that the delicate shifting mechanisms won't get bashed and put out of alignment. And the cables which operate the shifters also need to be kept moving freely if it's to work properly. It all adds up to rather more possible points of failure than a hub gear system, the need for a little more care, a bit of extra fiddling, and earlier replacement.

Having said that, component manufacturers have worked intensively on derailleur gearing in recent decades, taking full advantage of improvements in computer design technology and materials. Today's derailleurs are the best they've ever been, and if, like me, you use hub gears for everyday commuting and keep the derailleur bikes for weekends or tours, you'll get many years of use from a decent derailleur system.

Why derailleurs?

There's one area where derailleurs absolutely, completely, cannot be challenged by hub gears. That's affordable wide range. Even the cheapest 'mountain bike' will have triple chainrings and a reasonably wide-range sprocket set on the back wheel, giving a gearing range of close to 500%. Now unless you start buying a Rohloff hub (£500+) or combining multi-speed hub gears (say £150) with the Schlumpf Mountain-Drive (say

£250) there's just no realistic way to get that sort of range except with derailleurs. And at the really low end, for 20" gears and under, many of the non-Rohloff hub gears will be outside their manufacturers' recommended range – you risk breaking them with the high torque that low gears can generate.

So if you want to go touring, or even just have a hilly commute, a derailleur drivetrain is really the only sensible solution without serious investment. It's this factor more than any other which explains the derailleur's dominance in mountain biking. Thankfully, the intense development of MTB drive-trains has also benefited touring cyclists, who often apply the same components on-road.

Some riders just prefer derailleurs anyway – the feel of them, the easy fix-ability. A useful solution for 'round town' is a single front chainring and a wide-range rear cassette. This gives a useful gear range along with a fairly simple set-up.

How do derailleurs work?

As the name suggests, derailleurs simply 'de-rail' the chain, shoving it sideways so that it moves from one cog to the next as you pedal. Over the years, of course, the principle has been refined, but basically that's all any derailleur does.

Perhaps the most significant refinement has been indexed shifting,

meaning a 'click' for each gear. Previously you'd just rely on 'feel' to make changes, requiring rather more skill and judgement. But to achieve this decisive, intuitive action, the manufacturers had to make the system much more precise and tightly integrated. For each click of the shifter, the derailleur needs to move a very precise distance (which varies between manufacturers). As more and more sprockets have been added at the back the distance between them has shrunk, making tolerances even tighter. There's a jump between 5 to 8 speed systems, which use a sprocket spacing of around 5 mm (or just under) and the 9 and 10 speed systems, which go down to 4 mm or thereabouts. For less finicky adjustment it's a good idea to stick with 8 speeds or fewer.

Riding derailleurs

Running the chain from a small chainring at the front to a large one at the back gives low gears, and the 'large front' to 'small rear' gives high gears – taking you further per turn of the pedals. Usually the gears are laid out so that there are two or three chainrings at the front, with quite large size jumps between them, and then between 7 and 9 sprockets at the back, more closely spaced in size.

This typically means that for most of your riding you can stay in the middle ring at the front, and just use the other two rings occasionally. The gear-shifting process between chainrings is normally rather less slick than between cogs at the back (partly because the front changer has to shift the top run of the chain, which is under tension), so this avoids too much front shifting.

How you physically do the shift will depend very much on your particular set-up. Most systems are reasonably consistent, with clear buttons for 'up' and 'down'. Bar-end shifters, as used on many recumbents, offer instant tactile feedback about which gear you're in. Most  other types, including the popular twist shifters, have an indicator of some sort as a visual clue (often not much use at night…). After a while, you'll start to know instinctively which gear you're in.

The first 'law' of riding derailleurs is that you only shift while pedalling. On most derailleurs, attempting a shift when stopped just makes the derailleur attempt to bend the chain: it's the rolling action of the chain in motion which allows proper shifting. There are some derailleurs which let you 'pre-shift', 'storing' the cable motion in a spring until you pedal and the gear change is made. But it's best not to rely on that.

Pedalling backwards as you shift is likely to mangle your rear derailleur with potentially disastrous and expensive consequences. This vulnerability may not be obvious to novices so it's worth stressing.

There's one other 'law' to observe. Consider what happens when you move the chain across the sprockets at the back. The chain is fixed at the front (on the middle chainring, say) so it's forced to run at an angle on any except the middle rear sprocket. Although the chain is designed to accommodate this flexing, it does lose some efficiency when run at the more extreme angles. The issue is more serious when you're on the small or large chainrings at the front: if you run the chain all the way across (small-small or large-large) the angle is generally excessive. Also, you'll be at the extremes of what the chain tensioner built into the rear derailleur can handle, so the chain can end up tight (large-large) or slack (small-small). Most often the system will start to get noisy as you move into undesirable gear combinations – no disaster, just shift chainrings to fix it and then fine-adjust with the rear derailleur to match your speed.

TOP TIP: Quick links

One of the great derailleur inventions is the SRAM Powerlink chain link. This device makes it easy to break and re-assemble chains by hand – well worth fitting to all your derailleur chains, and have a few spares, too, for emergency chain repairs. Available from any dealer, and some other brands have equivalents too.

Derailleur decisions

The range of derailleur gearing out there seems mind-boggling. Shimano, SRAM, Campagnolo, Suntour and a host of others each have a slew of groupsets (complete packages of bike components) at all different price-points. And that's just the tip of the iceberg: many bike makers will use third-party components, often unbranded, to keep the cost down, from a myriad of Taiwanese, Korean or Chinese suppliers – which may be just as good as the name-brands anyway. There are also a huge number of 'niche' suppliers, offering everything from tandem-specific products to weight-saving replacement titanium bolts. To compound the problem, product ranges change every year, and new parts may or may not be compatible with old ones.

But it's not quite as overwhelming as it may seem. Broadly, derailleur systems divide into three groups:

» *'Road'* systems prioritise light weight, relatively high gears, and closely-spaced ratios. Examples include Shimano's Tiagra or Ultegra systems and just about everything by Campagnolo.

» *'MTB'* systems have a wide gear range from very low to not-particularly-high and are designed to cope with a certain degree of mud. Examples include Shimano's Deore or SRAM's 'X' series.

» *'Comfort'* cycling groupsets are designed for premium user-friendly town, touring and fitness bikes, especially perhaps for mainland Europe. Most, such as SRAM's i-Motion, employ hub gears, although Shimano's Nexave series is derailleur-based (with electronic shifting at the top end).

» *'Utility'* groupsets are for the cheap end of the market, usually MTB styled with triple chainrings but with fairly high ratios overall (as most non-enthusiast cycle users prefer a slow cadence). Shimano's Tourney groupset is at the top end of this category: most are unbranded. Built to a price-point but can work OK if you're lucky. If you're not, and especially if the frame is also badly aligned, cheap derailleur gears can be a nightmare to work on and may function marginally at best.

The compatibility trap

Most people get bikes already kitted out with a decent gearing system. The fun starts when it comes to replacing parts which have worn out. Making sure everything's compatible is especially critical when it comes to the rear derailleur: it really must move by precisely the right amount if the gears are to work properly. There's no space here to make even a start on the technical details of this: consult a good bike shop or check online at Sheldon Brown's comprehensive site (www.sheldonbrown.com).

The other common situation where you might end up buying derailleur parts is when you need higher or lower gears than are currently fitted to your bike. Again, the compatibility issue rears its ugly head: there are many, interlocking aspects of a properly-working derailleur system. If you want, say, a bigger top gear you might simply replace your outer chainring with a larger one, assuming one's available to fit your chainset – not always the case if you're wanting to run a large ring on an MTB crankset. If you need to replace the crankset then you need to get one designed for the length of bottom bracket you already have. Then, you'll certainly need to add links to the chain. And then you'll probably find that the front changer which worked well before can't cope with the larger ring – or rather, it can't cope with the range from small ring to large. The rear derailleur, too, might struggle to keep the chain tensioned over the now extended range of chainring sizes. And so it goes on…

Of course, many changes are straightforward. But if you choose to do it yourself rather than consult a dealer, do plenty of research first.

Other derailleur ideas and inventions

Elliptical chainrings

There have been repeated attempts over the years to match the pedal motion more precisely to human biomechanics – perhaps the simple, circular motion of a standard crankset just seems too simple to be optimal. An easy and lightweight way to 'tweak' the motion is to use elliptical or otherwise non-circular chainrings, the idea being that you get effectively a lower gear when the chain is pulling on the 'narrow' bit of the ellipse.

Though this approach has its fans, most riders seem to prefer simple round cranks. Nowadays elliptical rings are made by Highpath Engineering (www.highpath.co.uk) and ROTOR (see below). Highpath, incidentally, also supply custom-made cassettes to fit any current system, and also have a wealth of derailleur info on their website.

ROTOR cranks

Moving the cranks slightly out of phase rather than employing elliptical rings, the ROTOR crank system is somewhat expensive and complex. But it

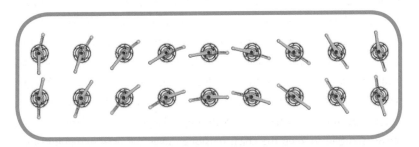

has been positively received, especially by recumbent riders, who reported real benefits in fatigue reduction and around 5% speed increase in hill-climbing, especially perhaps for those who ride with a lower cadence. See www.rotorbike.com

Auto-changing derailleurs

Cars have automatic transmissions – why not bicycles? Over the years there have been a number of attempts to automate the shifting process. Most commonly, mechanical systems are employed, with a series of weights attached to the rear wheel. As the bike speeds up, these fly outwards by centrifugal force, operating the rear derailleur via some linkage. In theory, it should choose a gear to match your speed. In practice, it has never been made to work well, with abrupt, unexpected shifting.

Shimano do have a much, much better automatic derailleur system on their flagship 'Comfort' groupset, Nexave C810. Both front and rear derailleurs are operated electronically via a computer controller and powered by a small hub dynamo in the rear wheel. Unfortunately this Nexave system is so expensive that it's rarely used even on high-end bikes.

Electronic shifting

The cables are certainly the weak point of any derailleur system, with excessive friction the number one cause of derailleur shifting problems. So there have been attempts to do away with the cables altogether. Shimano have one system (as above) and I recall another, clever one from Mavic. To avoid the use of heavy batteries or a hub dynamo, they designed the system to use the rider's own energy to accomplish the shifts. When a shift was required, a small solenoid-driven pin would shoot out and engage the chain just long enough to 'pull' the derailleur into its new position. It was all aimed at racing cyclists, but never caught on. Now, as I write this, electronic shifting is also about to return in the top-end racing groupsets from Shimano. It'll probably be a few years yet before the technology trickles down to price points of interest to practical cyclists.

Bicycle brakes

What makes a good brake?

Brakes are perhaps the most safety-critical system on a bike, so it's well worth understanding what they do and how.

For my money a good brake is one that stops you powerfully in all conditions without excessive finger pressure, gives good 'feel', and requires minimal maintenance. It's also lightweight, robust and reasonably priced.

» 'All conditions' might include an emergency stop for a stepped-out pedestrian, in the rain, while towing a trailer. Or maybe pulling up for a T-junction at the bottom of a mountain pass, carrying full touring gear, in the Mediterranean sun.

» 'Powerfully' means that it should be the tyre's grip or the cycle's stability which limits your braking, not the brake. This level of braking power may not be wise if you're not confident in modulating your braking – hence the 'limiters' on some SRAM and Shimano V and roller brakes, designed to prevent riders going over the bars with unintentionally strong braking. There are doubtless some who appreciate these systems, but I think most riders would rather have reserves of braking power and trust their reflexes to slack off if necessary.

» 'Without excessive finger pressure' means safety for riders without strong fingers, and comfort for anyone in demanding conditions. I remember many years ago making a two-hour descent in Corsica on a calliper-braked, steel-rimmed 'racer' with my fingers absolutely cramped up at the end of it: not good for safety or comfort. Modern brakes are so much better.

» 'Good feel' means a smooth comfortable brake lever, which pulls easily to a clear 'bite point', after which you can precisely control the degree of braking by finger pressure. Even with a powerful squeeze the lever shouldn't hit the handlebar. Ideally the brakes should behave the same in all weather conditions.

» 'Minimum maintenance' means having to fiddle with it as infrequently as possible. That includes replacement of pads, rims and other wearing parts. It's also good if the brake doesn't excessively impede wheel removal for puncture-fixing.

» 'Light weight' is relative: no heavier than most other brakes is good enough for me.

» 'Robust' means unlikely to be damaged by the everyday knocks of parking or transporting bikes. This addresses one of the few drawbacks of the disk brake, the easily-bent or bashed rotors!

» Price speaks for itself.

One further non-technical consideration is attractiveness to thieves. For my commuting and everyday 'hack' bike I've ruled out disk brakes mainly because they'll act as thief magnets. But as time goes on this is becoming less of an issue: cheap disk brakes are fairly common now even on supermarket bikes, so apart from the top brands they probably won't be over-tempting.

Modern braking systems come close to fulfilling all of these criteria. But unfortunately, the perfect brake doesn't exist – and perhaps it never can, as every design must compromise somewhere to accommodate the laws of physics.

So let's first take a look at some of the science of stopping, and see what it means for bicycle brakes in the real world.

The science of stopping

Braking energy

All brakes essentially do the same thing: they convert the energy of your motion into heat, and then dissipate that heat.

Any moving object has energy intrinsic to its motion. This energy could, for example, be used to lift weight against gravity, perhaps by rolling up a slope. Conversely, objects rolling down a slope gain energy from gravity.

So if you want to slow down or stop, the energy in your momentum must go somewhere. It's one of the basic rules of physics that energy can't be created or destroyed, just converted from one form to another.

Brakes convert energy into heat, normally using the friction of a brake pad on moving metal. That heats the brake up. But hot things necessarily transfer heat to their cooler surroundings, so the energy eventually just dissipates away into the atmosphere.

For normal, round-town riding the heating effect may not really be noticeable or significant, but for touring, MTBing or even if you just live somewhere hilly, it can really matter. If you're on a tandem with twice the mass to stop – and thus double the heat to dissipate – it's critical.

Temperatures can rise fast, and high. Don't try touching your brakes after a hard descent – try a little drop of water on the rims or brake rotor just to see. Quite often it'll fizz and boil off instantly. That means the rims are at well over 100°C.

The problem is that there's a limit to how hot a brake can get before the heat does some damage. So choosing a brake for demanding use is all about getting rid of heat safely.

Two things in particular promote good heat loss – a large surface area and good airflow. And the more mass (weight) there is, the lower the temperature rise for a given energy input.

Rim brakes are great for surface area – you have the whole rim to heat up, and there's plenty of air flowing around to cool it off. There's usually a fair amount of metal mass in the rim, too. Unfortunately if the rim does heat up excessively then the consequences can be disastrous – the inner tube heats up, the air in it expands from the heat, and the pressure build-up can explode your tyres.

I've actually seen this happen on a girlfriend's bike as we were touring in Norway years ago – thankfully no great harm done, but it split the tyre and inner tube. Ever since I've been careful to stop every so often on mountain downhills, if using a rim-braked bike, to pause to let things cool off a little. The smaller your wheels, the less surface and the less mass they have, so the quicker the rims will heat up. I'm very careful on my Birdy folding bike!

Brakes mounted at the wheel hub can generally get a lot hotter without causing serious damage, but the smaller area at the wheel centre means they're not as good at getting rid of heat. There's usually not as much material in a brake rotor or drum as there is in a rim, so it'll get hotter for the same energy input.

Disks tend to be much better than drums when it comes to heat dissipation as they have a larger area and are out in the air flow, and they can also withstand overheating well. But that's at the cost of having a relatively fragile rotor exposed on the side of the wheel, in contrast to the enclosed drums. For extreme braking, get the largest-diameter disk you can to maximise surface area and hence heat dissipation.

Riding techniques can help minimise brake heating – see later.

Braking leverage

Brakes are a lovely demonstration of the mechanical principle of levers. Pushing the brake pads against the rim with finger pressure would be useless, but when that same finger force is multiplied via the system of levers and cables which make up a braking system, it can exert very significant force indeed. The trade-off is that as force is multiplied, distance moved is divided. You can have movement or force but not both. More movement is nice, as it leaves clearance for dirt or wobbles when the brakes aren't applied.

Lower forces are also good for brake cables, especially round corners, which is why V-brakes are so successful. By using brake levers which pull more cable than the old cantilever brake levers, then using longer lever-arms on the brake itself, they allow the cable to slip through its housing under lower tension, causing less friction and improving feel, braking power and reliability. Most mechanical disk brakes use V-brake type levers for this same reason – lower cable tension.

Leverage also comes into play when you look at the wheel as a whole. Acting on the rim, a brake is effectively towards the end of a lever arm extending from the wheel axle to the ground, with the resistance force between tyre and ground near the same end. So the braking forces of rim brakes just have to create enough friction against the rim to match that resistance or a little more. This means there's enough motion to draw the pads back several millimetres, enough to clear any normal wobble in the rims.

But if the brake is at the wheel's hub, the length of the lever arm from axle to ground will be working against the brake, which is right near the axle end. So a much larger braking force will be needed for the same effect in slowing the bike. This is why hub brakes (disk and drum) work with very small running clearances: they need huge forces to create enough friction, so available motion is minimal. Incidentally the high forces do have one useful side effect – they squeeze out water very well, so disks tend to have no problem in the wet.

High forces aren't generally a desirable thing in lightweight structures like bicycles. Big forces tend to require plenty of metal to support them, and plenty of metal means heavy. This is one reason why rim brake systems tend to be lighter (and often cheaper) than disks or drums, and why they're still used on racing bikes.

Leverage also explains why hub brakes are more powerful in smaller wheels. Most drums and disks are designed for 26" or 28" wheels – put them in a 20" rim and the braking they'll generate will be around half as powerful again. This can be too much of a good thing, making the brakes lock up at the slightest pressure, so on most 20"-wheeled bikes or trikes where disk brakes are used, the smallest available rotor is fitted. The same effect means that drum brakes which are just too weedy on full size wheels are perfect for small-wheeled machines.

Braking dynamics

Activate your bicycle brakes and it'll slow the bike down – but your body wants to go right on moving. You'll be pushing at the handlebars to hold you in place. That pressure, plus a little from the bicycle's own weight, is what should limit how fast you can stop. Overdo it and the bike will pivot around its front wheel and tip you right over the front.

The same effect happens on any vehicle. If the tyres have enough grip and the brakes enough bite, you can do a 'stoppie' and lift the back wheels. It's not generally a good idea to do this on a bike as it seriously reduces your directional control.

But just before the rear wheel lifts, or front wheel skids, you can be confident that you're braking just as strongly as possible. It also demonstrates that for really stopping you, the front brake is the one that matters. As the rear has little or no weight on it in a hard stop, it can't contribute much to the braking anyway. And any attempt to use it would result in a skid – bad news for controlled steering.

The back brake does have some purpose of course – it's handy for gently scrubbing off speed, or in slippery conditions. If there's a decent amount of weight on the rear wheel, as there is with many folding bikes or recumbents, a good back brake can stop you reasonably well.

But make sure your front brake is up to scratch. It's the one that counts.

Recommended brakes

» *Round town:* If possible, choose hub brakes for low maintenance. If you are a fast rider, a rim brake on the front wheel and a hub at the back is a good combination, offering emergency stopping power plus a low-maintenance way to scrub off speed. I prefer a hydraulic Magura brake to normal V-brakes, but either is fine.

»   *On tour:* Rim brakes or disks: other hub options won't have the power. If you're paranoid about repairs, choose mechanical rather than hydraulic models.

»   *Heavy loads:* Hard to beat a large disk brake, although a set of Magura or good V-brakes can come close.

Braking techniques

Don't brake

Don't brake if you don't have to! Braking wastes away energy you've put in through the pedals, wears out your brakes and risks the tyre slipping. Instead, try to anticipate speed changes. Cultivate an energy-efficient riding style, coasting up to a halt rather than slamming on the brakes at the last minute. Adapt your speed to fit neatly into gaps in traffic or to match a traffic light sequence – it's a smoother, more efficient and relaxing way to ride.

Know your brakes

It's wise to know the limits of braking on the bike you're riding and bear it in mind. Leave yourself a way out if you're riding in traffic which could suddenly stop faster than you can. It can be better to steer out of trouble rather than brake, but be prepared for an emergency stop. Practice it somewhere safe.

Braking on long hills

Long hills are the hardest test of brakes, especially with a tandem or heavy load. The best strategy is to use your brakes as little as possible – sit upright in the saddle, using your body for air-braking, and put the pedals vertical to maximise your legs' wind resistance, too.

Let your speed rise, then brake hard for corners or just every so often, rather than dragging on the brakes all the way down. This limits heat build-up, mainly because the higher speeds mean that air resistance can do some of the work absorbing the energy of your descent, plus higher speeds cool brakes better. This does however require confidence.

Alternate use of front and rear brakes, so that each has at least a few moments to cool down between applications.

If it's a really long descent, play it safe and stop every so often and admire the view as you let the brakes cool off.

Bits of brake

Brake levers

Brake levers are mostly pretty good nowadays. I like a smooth alloy lever (plastic/composite may be lighter, but never feels as nice), which pivots easily in its mount without much sideways play. I also like a two-bolt mount, so that you don't have to slide the lever on from the end of the bars. A reach adjuster screw is good to fit those with smaller hands.

Many brake levers for flat bars nowadays have two alternative settings,

letting you fit the cable in two different ways: either for cantilevers or for V-brakes. The V-brake setting is always the one furthest from the lever pivot. Most mechanical disk brakes use this setting too. Brake levers should be fitted so that your wrist is straight in your normal riding position.

Hydraulic brake systems use their own lever designs, usually very good in my experience.

A neat way to add a hand position on drop bars is to use the Tektro RX2 bar-top lever, available via dealers, or look online:

Another one of note is a double-pull lever for special needs or trike use, available from e.g. Mission Cycles. www.mission-cycles.co.uk

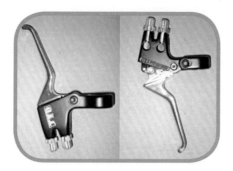

Cables

The standard bicycle brake cable was developed from the Bowden cable, designed originally to activate aircraft controls. The inner cable slides inside

an outer cable formed from square wire wrapped tightly round, often lined inside and out with plastic. The outer can bend but it can't compress, so any relative motion of outer and inner at one end is reproduced at the other. The ones without a liner require grease or oil lubrication. But if you can, buy the better plastic-lined ones with stainless inner cables. No lubrication is required and they have a much nicer feel.

Even more expensive but good are 'Goretex' lined cables, and users report much reduced friction.

Another very nice system is NOKON cables, which replaces the wrapped wire outer with a series of aluminium segments with spherical ends. Very pretty, very light and very flexible. But pricey.

Hoses

Replacing the mechanical cable with hydraulic hose has particular benefits for twisty or long cable runs. In a Bowden cable the friction adds up with every bend, and finger pressure expended overcoming that friction won't make it to the brake. Hydraulics simply don't have that problem. They're also more or less maintenance free – although if something does go wrong they're much harder to fix.

The brake itself

Disk brakes

Disk brakes are great: powerful, weather-resistant and, especially in the hydraulic versions, require very little finger pressure to stop you. There are plenty of good brands around – Hope still seem to be top of the tree for hydraulics, and Avid BB7s and Shimano's models are respected mechanicals, but there are plenty more good ones besides.

Minor drawbacks to disks include the ease with which the rotors can be slightly bent causing an annoying rub, the often rather fiddly pad change procedures, and squeal in the wet. They're also rather too attractive to thieves.

Drum brakes

Drum brakes are made currently by Sturmey-Archer and SRAM, and I'm afraid I find them mediocre at best. For me, a fairly heavy and fast rider, they're just not powerful enough to consider seriously on a front wheel.

In all I've tried, a hard pull on the lever just doesn't provide the grab you need for an emergency stop, more a gradual slow! They can work well as a rear brake, though, and many more sedate and, perhaps, lighter riders do find their braking satisfactory. Certainly in smaller wheels, like the 20" ones often used on folding bikes or recumbents, they're just fine, as this effectively gives them better leverage.

Drum brakes have a lot of advantages otherwise: they're very low maintenance, robust, and aren't sensitive to weather. It's a pity nobody makes a really powerful one nowadays.

One special-purpose drum brake which is very good is the Arai drag brake for tandems, designed with plenty of metal to soak up heat on long descents. It really is effective and reliable. Consult tandem specialists for more details.

Trike makers Greenspeed (www.greenspeed.com.au) make a special narrow hub brake for Brompton folding bikes – a great idea, very effective in the small wheels, and available from them or their UK distributor, Westcountry Recumbents (www.wrhpv.com)

The Arai drum brake for tandems

Roller brakes

Shimano's hub brake uses metal rollers running against a hardened ring to provide the friction, and it's quite effective. Certainly it has more than enough bite for a back wheel, but like drums it may not have all the power

you really need for a front brake. Roller brakes do apparently burn up their internal grease if overheated on long descents, and without the grease they can be ferociously effective to the point of locking your wheel.

iBrake

SRAM's 'next-generation' hub brake is a narrow-profile drum brake

which attaches to the hub (rather than being built-in, like the Sturmey models). So it's available for both front and rear, if you can find any compatible hubs – not easy in the UK. Unfortunately it has never been available as an after-market accessory, and it has been fitted to precious few bikes as original equipment. It's an interesting alternative, so let's hope that they make it more widely available soon.

Side and centre pull brakes

This type of brake was the standard for touring for many years, and still is for racing bikes. Also seen, especially on kids' bikes, as the cheapest and nastiest brakes imaginable.

Sidepulls work well on racing bikes with thin tyres and narrow clearance, as the pads aren't cantilevered out too far from the bolt supporting the brake above the tyre. But on a fatter tyred bike the arms get long and flexible and put a lot of stress on the pivot bolt. The result is ineffectual, squashy brakes. Why do manufacturers do this? Because it's cheaper to drill a single hole through the fork crown to fit sidepulls than it is to weld on the bosses for a V-brake.

This short-arm sidepull provides effective braking on a Mezzo folding bike.

So unless it's a shiny, rigid short-arm model for a racing bike, steer clear of side-pulls.

Canti, V and U brakes

Mountain bikes pushed the development of better brakes. U-brakes, cantilever brakes and finally V-brakes were the result. All working on bosses firmly fixed to the bike frame, they tend to flex much less than the old side or centrepull designs, offering better braking force and feel, and accommodating fat tyres without a problem. V-brakes raised the bar still further with their reduced cable tension design. Performance of all but the cheapest is usually very good.

Diminishing returns apply with V-brakes after you're out of the cheap and nasty price-point territory: I can't see how the very pricey units will perform very much better than a basic set, apart from shaving a few grams or looking prettier. The one exception is 'parallel push' types, which have an additional linkage to keep the brake pads parallel to the rim, giving more even wear, easier adjustment and better performance.

Magura brakes

My favourite when it comes to rim brakes are these German-made hydraulic stoppers. Splendidly low maintenance, lovely feel. Also available in discreet black. The only real downside is that like all rim brakes they wear away your rims with time. Refilling them in the event of a hose breakage is a fiddle – but it so rarely happens, and the rest of the time they're a delight. For utility use the budget HS11 model is perfectly adequate: the more popular HS33 does have nicer

levers though. A version for drop bars, the HS66, is sadly discontinued but has a devoted following among touring tandem riders, and used ones trade for high prices on eBay.

Even more brakes

As I can't write a whole book on brakes and must limit this to one chapter, we'll have to miss out coaster (back pedal) brakes, the specific issues of braking on tandems or trailers, and some of the interesting alternative braking systems which have been invented over the years, such as band brakes, electrical and mechanical regenerative brakes, anti-lock braking systems for bicycles and more… maybe next time!

Other bike bits

Handlebars

There are only five points where you, the rider, typically touch your bike as you ride: two handgrips, two pedals and the saddle. On an upright bike the handlebar and grips are especially important: you're often leaned over to some extent, throwing a significant proportion of your weight onto your wrists. If you don't get the bars and grips right, wrist pain will eventually follow.

The bars you choose are a personal preference of course, but for practical reasons most transport cyclists go for flat bars these days, rather than racing-style drop bars. Gear and brake components commonly used for

utility cycling (in contrast to road-racing) fit on flat bars but not on drops (the tubing is the wrong diameter). It's also generally easier to fit mirrors, bells and the like to flat bars than to drops.

I personally find that straight, flat bars are hard on the wrists: 'riser' bars are rather better, with an upward, backwards sweep. But both are improved enormously by adding a set of ergonomic grips, which help support the wrist and palm of the hand. My favourites are the Ergon models (www. ergon-bike.com), not cheap at around £20/pair, but worth every penny in comfort. Most bikes shops will be able to get them via Extra UK.

If you don't get on with the handlebars your bike came with, or they seem too low, or too far forwards or back, don't just suffer in silence! Changing the bars or their position is a straightforward and relatively inexpensive job which any bike shop will undertake if you don't fancy it yourself. If you'd like some old-fashioned 'sit up and beg' bars, these are available too. If your bike shop can't find them, HubJub has a top quality, if pricey, selection at www.hubjub.co.uk.

Saddles

Again, personal preferences rule! For some time I used a selection of whatever saddles my bike came with, and really, if your cycle rides are just

short urban hops, this may not be a problem. I was then happy for years with a Rido plastic saddle, cunningly shaped to distribute the pressure – see www.rido-cyclesaddles.com. At just a tenner plus postage it's cheap, wipe-clean, and lasts for ages.

But I'm now, finally, a convert to Brooks saddles, those leather icons of

cycling. For me, on longer touring-style riding they beat everything except a recumbent. The standard B17 (or the B17 S for ladies) works well for me, and is the cheapest in the range – around £40 currently. Choose the Flyer (pictured, around £50) if you'd like a little extra comfort: the springs at the back add a very noticeable cushioning effect. The need to cover the leather in the rain does make the Brooks less practical for an everyday errand-running bike, though.

Carrier racks

If you only carry light loads by bike you can get away with a rucksack or

courier bag. For anything more panniers are much more pleasant. With the weight on the bike, not on your back, you'll breathe easier, be better ventilated and just feel more relaxed.

As to the racks themselves, if possible try to avoid the 'clip-on' type of rear rack which attaches to the seatpost – these put more stress on an already heavily-loaded part, and often have very low permissible loads. Better by far is a rack which attaches either side of the frame near the rear axle, and up top on the seat stays. This gives a strong, stable mount, usually rated to carry at least 25 kg, though some go well beyond that (with some safety margin, too). There are many good models from £25 upwards, but if you want the best go straight to models by Tubus (available widely via dealers) or Old Man Mountain (in the UK via Carradice: www.carradice.co.uk). My personal favourite is the very heavy duty Tubus Cargo, at around £65.

Chaincases

Chains are usually oily, dirty or both. They're also placed inconveniently close to the cuffs of your trousers. Cycle clips, or tucking your trousers into your socks, are both possible solutions. Luckily, there's another, better way, which is to tuck the chain away behind a nice, solid barrier.

On bikes this generally takes two forms: either a chain guard which just covers the top run of the chain (and so protects your trousers) or a full chaincase, which encloses the whole chain. This more elaborate design keeps the chain completely clean, considerably prolonging its life.

Sadly, in the UK the only bikes fitted with full chaincases tend to be imports from Germany or the Netherlands, often rather heavy (but very reliable) roadster-type machines. Just a few rather pricey 'performance' models are now appearing: see for example the Vector from Koga (www.koga.com) or the T-400 Rohloff imported by Bikefix (www.bikefix.co.uk). Only hub gear or single-speed bikes are generally suitable for fitting chaincases.

Both of the models named above use a very particular chaincase, the Hebie Chainglider (pictured opposite). This can be bought separately (around £30) to fit many hub gear bikes: it's just a system of flexible plastic shells which snap together around your chain. But it only fits certain chainring and sprocket sizes: check at www.hebie.com or via the UK importers: www. amba-marketing.co.uk. It's a neat, light system which adds very little friction, and I recommend it highly.

Lights

If you use your bike for practical cycling all year round, lights are a necessity. I've tried a succession of battery and dynamo-powered systems over the years, and it's heartening how far the technology has advanced. LEDs are now ubiquitous, thankfully, in all but the cheapest lights.

The choice between batteries and dynamo is a tricky one. If you ride much on unlit roads, or off-road, then a high-powered battery system is probably called for. For just occasional use in lit urban streets a couple of small clip-on battery lights might suffice.

Where dynamo lights come into their own is when you're riding regularly at night, but without needing truly extreme levels of illumination. This covers many riders' winter commuting and transport cycling. A decent dynamo system will be plenty bright, highly reliable and completely hassle-free – no lights to remember to remove (or lose to thieves), and no recharging routine to remember.

If at all possible, forget side-running dynamos: modern ones aren't bad but aside from the initial cost, hub dynamos are simply better: they never slip, whine annoyingly, or get knocked out of alignment. Hub dynamos are also noticeably more efficient, so there's less drag slowing you down. Counter-arguments are that they may be slightly heavier, and there can be some drag even when they're switched off. But I find the drag undetectable even when the lights are on, so don't worry about it!

You need to get a hub dynamo built into a wheel (or do it yourself) but once that's done you have a system which is unobtrusive, unaffected by the weather and quite theft-resistant.

Hub dynamos are available from Shimano (from around £55), SRAM (also from £55, but less easily available), Sturmey (£55ish, with drum brake) and SON (from £130ish, but very nice). I've never been able to tell much

difference in drag between models, so unless you're bothered by weight pretty much any recent model will do fine.

For the lights, the Busch und Mueller range is reliably good quality and available via most bike shops. Choose LED light units with the 'Senso plus' functions: this means they stay on when you stop, and also switch on automatically when it gets dark. Once you've used this system you'll never go back: the lights just do their job without you having to even think about it.

If you want the ultimate dynamo front light (for £90+) then look up the SON Edelux at www.sjscycles.co.uk. Perfect for longer night rides on unlit roads, but overkill for most users.

Town bikes

Introduction

Cycling for transport is what this book is all about, and in this section we'll run through some tricks and tips – and equipment – which can make getting around by bike that bit easier. The focus is on urban commuting-type journeys, which includes all sorts of errand-running and general utility cycling where the object is to get from A to B with as little fuss as possible.

Bike benefits

Choosing to do my utility travel by bike is easy for me – I don't drive, and I live in York, where getting about by bike is relatively pleasant. The places I need to go regularly are within easy riding distance. So most of the time, it's an appropriate and easy way to get around.

For others, though, circumstances may be very different. I lived for several years in London, and that's a whole different cycling challenge, as

are the narrow lanes of Cornwall, or the hilly terrain of Bristol, for example. The layout of the place you live, traffic conditions, climate and the sort of journeys you make can all influence the practicality of cycling. Each of us will find our own 'comfort level' at which the benefits of cycling outweigh the often very real disincentives.

I hope it's still useful to describe what, for me, are the main benefits of transport cycling:

» *Convenience.* There are very few destinations where I have to worry about parking my bike, so the journey is door to door. Back at home, while neighbours struggle to find a place to park their car, I just go straight in to the shed at the back. There's no waiting for buses or taxis – no wasted time.

» *Independence.* On a bike I'm in complete control of where and when I travel – and am self-sufficient even in the case of mechanical problems. There's no relying on others or on public transport. It's no problem to get home at two in the morning if need be.

» *Speed.* On a bike I can get past traffic jams, take short-cuts and generally get around town efficiently at any time of the day or night. Rush hour has little effect on journey times.

» *Fitness.* Transport cycling is my only regular exercise and keeps me reasonably fit and healthy. It's 'free' exercise which just happens as part of the daily routine, with no special effort required.

» *Economy.* No fuel and garage bills for me – and my occasional spending on bike parts and servicing is a drop in the ocean compared to what my car-owning friends pay out on their transport. This isn't actually a primary motivation for me to cycle – and I spend more than I have to on bikes and accessories – but it's a very welcome side-effect.

» *Conviviality.* In a small town like York it's good to be able to stop and say hallo to friends you meet as you're out and about. It's nice to be in touch with your surroundings. Or if there's some interesting street show going on or whatever, it's easy to stop, wheel your bike over and take a look. You're part of the community on a bike.

» *Elegance.* I find cycling is an elegant and appropriate solution to getting me around town. Cars, coaches, trains and planes are all appropriate and (occasionally!) elegant solutions to different sorts of journey and I use them when necessary. But using the minimal and most efficient mode of transport for each trip has an aesthetic and perhaps moral appeal for me. Others couch their preference for cycling in the language of environmentalism, or of anti-car activism, and I can see where they're coming from. But my attachment to utility cycling isn't 'anti' anything or particularly ideologically-based – it's just a demonstrably good solution to getting around town, with few downsides for either the cyclist or wider society.

Alongside the positives are a number of downsides and limitations:

» *The weather.* Riding in the rain is rarely as bad as it seems as you're sat indoors looking out, but in truth it's often not pleasant. Even the best rain-wear is a bother to put on, take off and dry out. Being in touch with the elements can be a mixed blessing.

» *Traffic.* Although safe and assertive riding can make riding in traffic really quite safe, busy and cycle-unfriendly roads can make cycling much less of a pleasure. Riding at rush hour can raise stress levels too as drivers get frustrated.

» *Longer journeys.* The growth of out-of-town shopping and industrial estates has in many places made many people's journeys to work and for food ever longer and on nastier roads, making the cycling option less attractive over time.

» *Limited capacity.* Although trailers and panniers can work wonders, even a small car can safely carry more weight than one can on a bike. Then again, loads bigger than a weekly food shop are relatively rare. With children, it may take some ingenuity and investment to keep cycling (see the 'Family' chapter).

» *Image.* In some quarters cycling has an image problem, and it may not seem appropriate to turn up sweaty or wet at a smart destination. In reality, it is possible to cycle and remain presentable. Anyway, you'll look better and more attractive as a fit cyclist than you would as an unfit, passive passenger.

Theft prevention

If you're not lucky enough to have good, secure parking at each end of your journey then theft and vandalism is a big issue. In fact, it's *the* issue which determines the sort of bike you'll ride for most journeys.

In over 20 years of cycling – three of them in London – I've never had a bike stolen. Certainly there's some luck involved, but also some good planning and technique. Here's how I minimise the risk:

» Ride a hack bike! Do this whenever you're parking anywhere unsafe. A 'hack bike' is one that looks like rubbish, and so is unattractive to thieves, yet is mechanically sound. Unattractive doesn't necessarily mean cheap or nasty – it could be a nice, highly functional bike – and we'll go into some technical ideas later. But this concept is key to not losing your bike. Thieves will generally steal what's saleable – and that usually means anything reasonably new, or with components which can be 'recycled' for cash. Anything uncool, old-looking and dirty is less likely to be nicked. Combine it with a good lock and they'll generally just move on to an easier, more worthwhile target.

'Blackie' is a rebuilt Kona MTB frame, painted an anonymous black, fitted with good bits (DeoreXT). Old plumber's lagging, frayed duct tape, and faded fake leopard skin covering, contribute to a cheap, make-do appearance. The battered, sagging, obviously flimsy wooden vegetable box, and the unsightly tangle of aluminium tubing comprising a rear carrier rack, are master strokes -- no one wants this mess. The irony is that the box is very lightweight, and the unsightly tubing is aircraft grade; expensive, lightweight, and strong. Blackie is a fast, strong bike, yet does not look like much; sort of like a healthy mutt – Richard Ballantine.

» Some people advocate the opposite approach. Ride a town bike so extraordinarily nice and expensive that it's very distinctiveness is a deterrent. Thieves find it easier to pass on a 'normal' bike, so may pass up something expensive-looking if it's not a standard MTB or racing bike. I'm not completely convinced.

»   In any case, get a really good lock. A sufficiently determined thief will get through almost anything – what you're trying to achieve is deterrence. If the bike doesn't seem worth much, no thief will bother fighting their way through a serious lock to get it.

For many years my favourite was the Abus Granit 2000, an armoured cable lock costing about £60 and weighing over 2kg. It has the advantage over a D-lock of being able to fit around all sorts of bulky lampposts and the like. Forget most cheaper cable locks – they're not up to the job. After losing that lock I decided to go for something (slightly) lighter, and spent about the same on a good D-lock.

For belt and braces, use two locks of different types! Thieves would have to come equipped to defeat both.

If you have to lock the bike at one end of a regular commute, then you may be able to leave a truly massive lock (perhaps a motorbike

type) at your usual parking space, assuming it won't cause a nuisance.

The lock you carry with you has to be convenient, so you'll use it each and every time you stop. I've yet to find a really good frame mount for my lock, so it usually ends up hanging from the handlebars. If you do this make sure it's wedged in place between lamp brackets or something, so it can't shift and throw off the steering. Also, watch that it can't get stuck between stem and frame as you steer – this can be seriously dangerous.

» Park your bike well. Even if it means a short walk I always lock my bike to something solid in a public place – the busier the better. Be considerate to pedestrians, pram-pushers and the like who will need to get by. If you can park it next to other, nicer and less well-secured bikes that's even better.

If the best that's on offer is those front wheel-bending loop type stands, either move on and find somewhere better or if not busy, park

sideways along them and lock through the frame. Locking to the easily-removed front wheel only is an invitation for the rest of the bike to be stolen.

» Get rid of quick-releases. Quite often I can't arrange to put the D-lock through both front wheel and frame. With a quick-release (QR) axle your front wheel is then vulnerable to theft. To avoid this I either get a cheap front wheel with axle nuts or use a stainless steel hose clamp to secure the quick release shut. That way I can still get it off if need be, but it's a long enough job to deter the opportunist thief. An even quicker fix is to thread a cable tie through the QR – this is more easily cut, but is still an extra stage of deterrence. Saddle QRs should of course be replaced by a bolt, too.

Security QRs are also available, which replace the standard items

with ones that can only be opened with a special key. Pitlock and Pinhead systems are two good ones, and a set for both wheels and seatpost will cost £30-40. Most bike shops will have them, and it could be money well spent.

I've always found motion-activated cycle alarms more trouble than they're worth for everyday use. I'm rarely within hearing distance of my parked bike, anyway. They do have some uses for touring, though, where they offer some peace of mind at little weight penalty.

Of course, if you do have secure parking each end, you're free to ride what you like – the latest Rohloff-equipped recumbent if you fancy, or a fast road bike. But if not, a well-locked, anonymous and scruffy hack bike is your best bet that it'll still be there, ready to take you home.

Advanced cycling

Cycling isn't all that simple. Although millions seem to manage without any training, it's clear to me that cycling in traffic is a skill that needs learning. Once it's learned, though, it becomes an unconscious pleasure. One of the joys of cycling is flirting with the traffic, moving fast and efficiently to your destination without stress or incident.

There are as many ways and styles of riding as there are cyclists. My mother, for example, rides slowly up the side of the road, gets off and walks at every junction, and finds this a low-stress, safe and comfortable way to get around. I prefer to move fast with the traffic, take road space where necessary, and ride predictably and within the law.

Safe cycling encompasses a whole range of skills, and it's not easily communicated on paper. I will say, though, that in my view the most important skill for the advanced cyclist is empathy and anticipation. By this I mean constant awareness of the scene around you, and concerning yourself not only your own safe progress but with that of all of the traffic and pedestrians in the vicinity.

So if I hear a car coming up behind I'm already scanning the road ahead for where that car's going to overtake. I'm putting myself in that driver's position – when will he or she first spot me? Will there be room to swing wide – or will they be worried about the next bend or an oncoming car? Back to me, and what I can do about the situation. Should I move out to prevent them overtaking before it's safe? What's

my escape route if that kid playing with the ball lets it run out onto the road? Could there be another child behind that parked van?

All of this runs through the mind semi-consciously. On low-hazard stretches of road I day-dream happily, but a bend, the sound of a motor, or even just a pothole trigger that hazard awareness. Other experienced cyclists say the same – you develop a sixth sense of danger, and adjust your position, your speed, your attitude to avoid it. It gets easier as you get to know your particular journey, the phases of the traffic lights, the places where cars can pull out of concealed driveways.

Patience helps too. If I suspect from engine tone or close overtaking that a driver is impatient or aggressive, I'll wait behind at a junction rather than filter up to the front of the queue. It's safer to have such drivers in front of you.

Overall I feel aware enough to be in control – and thus safe, certainly safer than I feel as a car passenger. Utility cycling becomes that much more attractive and useful when you can go about it with confidence and without stress.

Teaching riding

When I first started cycling I was rather a bookish teenager, and devoured voraciously all that the local library could offer. Luckily, their cycling section contained two books which together are, I believe, largely responsible for my almost accident-free cycling career.

The first is *Richard's Bicycle Book* (ISBN 0-330-37717-5). Along with a wealth of good advice is a fine section on techniques for riding in traffic.

The second book goes into more detail – it's *Cyclecraft* by John Franklin (ISBN 0-11-702051-6). Reading this gave me knowledge and confidence in traffic and started me off with good habits.

A more recent 'must read' is *City Cycling* by Richard Ballantine (ISBN 9781905005604), a companion book in this series and a fantastic primer for any urban cyclist.

In many places there's now an additional source of guidance – adult cycle training. In the UK the CTC (www.ctc.org.uk or 0870 873 0060) is rolling out a widespread programme to be offered by local authorities. Many cycle campaign groups also offer either tuition or 'bike buddy' schemes, which pair up newcomers with experienced cycle commuters.

There are also private schools springing up – the two I know are both in London, and do work for local authorities as well as taking on individual customers: the London School of Cycling (www.londonschoolofcycling.co.uk or 020 7249 3779) and Cycle Training UK (www.cycletraining.co.uk or 020 7582 3535).

Transport cycling technology

Hack bikes

The 'hack bike' is a much-underestimated tool. Originally the term just meant a winter training bike for road racers, but it has come to mean any machine which is used for mundane riding when the 'posh bike' isn't

appropriate. For the utility cyclist, it has a very particular meaning.

First things first – forget all of the strange and wonderful bikes we feature elsewhere in this book. One quality of a hack bike is anonymity, and that means a boring, standard diamond frame upright bike. This is a matter of personal safety as much as anything – riding through certain parts of London, or any big city, it's safest just to blend in.

Old touring machines can be great hack bikes – anything with drop handlebars is good. A good-quality first-generation MTB frame can be a fine choice too. If you're really keen on theft prevention, a ladies' frame is extra-uncool.

The key is to achieve the 'just pulled from a skip' look without compromising performance. As this bike will be ridden in traffic it needs reliable brakes, gears to match the terrain, mudguards for the rain and lights if you'll be riding at night.

Lights are easy enough to add: there are plenty of good systems on the market which click on or off in an instant, or there are reliable modern dynamo options: these are permanently attached and I've never heard of theft being an issue. Mudguards are straightforward too – they'll lose that overly-new look after the first wet ride.

A fine hack. Grey ladies' frame is unattractive, but it's a decent ride with hub gears, cantilever front brake and a Magura brake at the back.

Almost by definition no manufacturer makes new hack bikes. A proper 'hack' takes a few years to mature with little add-ons like surplus lamp brackets and scuff-marks, and a scratched old carrier rack, all fitting it out as a tool for the owner's particular transport needs. A thing of beauty to the practical cyclist, the layers of grime are badges of honour for all-weather miles travelled.

Hack bike gears

Gears and brakes must work well while looking rubbish – this is no easy task. Derailleurs are not my favourite here – with a dirty, oily chain they can look scruffy enough, but the maintenance gets irksome.

Some riders go for the radical alternative: single-speed or fixed gear (single speed, but with no freewheel). I'm not a fan – I like my gears, so that I have the right ratio for acceleration away from traffic lights. Fixed does have some anti-theft advantages: most thieves will crash after a few yards.

The way to go is hub gears. Either find a new bike with them fitted, and 'distress' it enough to qualify as a hack bike, or retro-fit to an existing frame. One with horizontal dropouts will make this easier. As to which hub gear to choose, it depends on your terrain and preference, as we explained in an earlier chapter.

Hack bike brakes

There's no perfect solution to hack bike braking. The best-performing option – disk brakes – is out as too nickable. V-brakes are becoming so ubiquitous that a cheapish set is OK theft-wise. Old-style cantilever brakes are out of fashion, which is good, and they work well enough too. Even less attractive to criminals is any sort of calliper brake, such as you'd find on some older tourers.

The low-maintenance options – drum brakes and roller brakes – I find generally a bit weedy for front brake use as explained earlier, though they're a natural choice on the back wheel. If you're a lighter rider, or a generally sedate one, you may find them fine.

So what to use on the front? On my bike I've gone for the bottom-of-

the-range HS11 Magura hydraulic rim brakes. Although somewhat nickable, they're a discreet black and silver when new – and blend in quite well when filthy. They're low-maintenance, and pad replacement is easy. As an extra bonus, they make removing the front wheel that bit more difficult, too – with the tyre inflated it won't come out unless you know how to release the brakes.

Is there a gap in the market for a really powerful front drum brake? I'd certainly buy one…

Distressing your bike

Bike not looking old enough? There's no real substitute for a life of hard knocks to give a frame that lived-in look, but one method of making it look

nasty in a hurry is to do a very rough paint job with black 'Hammerite' paint. Then, don't clean it, and you'll soon have the utility bike every commuter – and no thief – would be proud of!

Puncture protection

Tyre manufacturers are getting ever better at puncture prevention – it's worth spending a little money to get a branded urban tyre from the likes of Schwalbe, Vredestein or Continental. Tyre weight does make a perceptible difference when accelerating, and better tyres do tend to be lighter.

For my town bike, even with good tyres, I add another layer of protection by filling the inner tubes with Slime sealant (available at most bike shops or car suppliers). This is a sort of green-coloured goo that lives in your inner tubes. If there's a puncture, the escaping air draws the Slime into the hole, which it then blocks up and seals.

You need Schraeder (car-style) valves to get the stuff into your tubes, but it's a simple enough process and the results are excellent – I can hardly remember the last time my Slimed tyres had a puncture that needed more than a few strokes of the pump to fix.

TOP TIP: Supermarket strategy

Doing a supermarket shop by bike? Save plastic bags – and time – by taking a pannier or two with you. Pick up a trolley, and put the panniers in it. Do your shopping. At the checkout, hook the panniers onto the side of the trolley and load everything straight in. Roll the trolley out to your bike, and lift the full panniers straight onto the carrier rack. Done! No plastic bags wasted, no heavy bags to carry.

Non-hack city bikes

If you're in the happy position of having secure parking at each end of your journey, then you're free to enjoy some very fine town bikes indeed.

Ideally, check out your local dealer first, as it's always good to buy local and benefit from their service backup. Ranges change regularly, so the models we've picked out below may not remain current. You'll also want to make your choice in light of the earlier chapters on brakes and gears: with this in mind most of the models I've picked out are hub geared. Of course, you're always free to use a racer, touring bike, folder or even a recumbent around town if you fancy – but these are bikes made for the job.

Traditional roadsters

For a flat town and a relaxed riding style, there's nothing at all wrong with a traditional three-speed – if you can find one! Three-speed hub gears seem thin on the ground in UK shops: most bikes on offer have basic derailleur systems, and some of these are good value, especially if you need the gears for a hilly commute. For example, the Trek T30 is fairly light and comes fully equipped with decent rack and mudguards for around £250.

If you do go for a three-speed hub gear, you'll get a narrower gearing range but also reliability and low maintenance. One example offered by one of my local bike shops is the Ridgeback Metro at around £280, or find a Dawes dealer and try the Haarlem 2008 model: again with rack and mudguards, it's around £290 with a light aluminium frame. Or for something more traditional see the Dawes Diploma range with their black-painted

steel tubes, full chaincases and retro looks, for much the same price. Or for around £400, the Giant Expression N7 may be worth seeking out – it has a seven-speed hub gear,   rack   and mudguards.

And check out your local shop for other brands – there are quite a few out there.

Cheaper bikes are available of course, but £250ish is probably a good basic price for a quality bike. Much less and the weight and poor quality components will still be a misery long after any supposed saving is forgotten.

Dutch-style upright bikes

A number of dealers are now offering ranges of bikes imported from mainland Europe, mostly the Netherlands. These tend to have a very upright riding position, full chaincase, be very solidly built (the Dutch expect their bikes to last!) and to therefore come in at slightly higher prices, from say £400ish to as high as you want to go.

These can make superb reliable machines, but won't suit all riders. Their weight and usually relatively limited gear range means they can be hard work on hills. The very upright riding posture is great for a relaxed neck and back, with hardly any weight on the wrists. It also looks very dignified. Unfortunately being bolt upright isn't much fun in a headwind,

and I personally find such bikes frustratingly slow, but if you're a relaxed rider you should definitely give one a try. The same applies if you're very tall: so are a number of Dutch people, and many bikes come in XXL sizes.

Importers include Amstel Cycles (www. amstelcycles.com. Tel 01903 730089) for Batavus bikes, Amsterdammers in Brighton for various brands   new and secondhand (www.amsterdammers.co.uk,   01273   571

555), and Cambridge Dutch Bikes (www.dutchbike.co.uk, 07772 738 899). Another major Dutch manufacturer, Gazelle, has a long list of UK dealers at www.gazelle.co.uk.

Fast hub-geared bikes

A number of bikes have been launched this year with 'urban' mountain bike styling, disk brakes front and back, and Shimano hub gears, often the Alfine hub. They're usually supplied 'bare', but make a fine basis for a town bike: just add rack, mudguards and lighting.

One such is the £580 Dahon Cadenza, which also has the bonus of folding, and comes ready-fitted with Big Apple tyres. There's also the

Ridgeback Genesis (£599),   the Trek Soho, (with roller brakes not disks,   around   £599), Cannondale Bad Boy (£850) and no doubt more.

High-end town bikes

In recent years a number of manufacturers have started offering premium town bikes, ready-equipped with quality components for practical cycling. This is a really useful development: instead of getting a bike and buying all of the accessories at full retail, you can get a bundle pre-assembled and ready to ride.

And if you're like me, you will want good components on your everyday bike. 'Must haves' for me now include a hub dynamo lighting system, hydraulic brakes, a full chaincase, wide-range hub gearing and a quality carrier rack and mudguards. Plus fat tyres and comfy grips and saddle.

Possible examples include the £1125 Vector from Koga, a modern town bike with integrated lighting, chaincase, Ergon grips and more; the only drawback is the 'designer' rear rack which isn't good for big loads. Or look at the Fahrrad-Manufaktur range imported by Bikefix: their T400 pretty much has it all, in derailleur (£875) or Rohloff (£1600) versions. Another model I like is the Cannondale Vintage 8, a very stylish and light machine with black-and-leather classic looks, dynamo lighting, Alfine hub, Chainglider, etc.

Even more is possible, at a price of course. Many bike shops will customise a bike to your requirements, or you can take advantage of the custom-build systems now available from at least two mainland Europe

The Cannondale Vintage 8

suppliers, via their UK dealers. Both Koga-Miyata and Santos Bikes from the Netherlands now have website-based systems which let you assemble your machine from a selection of frames, forks and quality components, with running totals of cost and weight. You can do this from home, or at a dealer, and the bike is then custom-made for you in the specification you've requested. See www.koga.com and www.santosbikes.com for dealer lists or to try it out.

Cruisers and style

If you live somewhere where it doesn't rain a lot, and you enjoy being seen around town, why not just ride a fantastic looking bike? It's all very well getting a super-functional, ultra-reliable bike for everyday use, but there's also something to be said for a bike which is just plain fun. If your use tends to the occasional, and you have secure parking, why not put form over function?

There are no end of them out there, from heavy, cheap cruisers to elaborate low-riders. For a good cruiser try the Pashley Tube Rider, or for low-riders see www.ridelow.co.uk.

Pictured here is a custom-built Santos SUB specified as an over-the-top, functional cruiser, with Rohloff gearing, Magura brakes and many other quality components. Lovely, but the best part of £2000....

Folding bikes

Why choose a folding bike?

Folding bikes are problem-solvers: they bring the benefits of cycling where a full-sized machine just wouldn't fit. This could be when your journey involves a combination of transport modes – such as car, train or bus – or where there's a lack of secure parking, or just a lack of space, at the ends of your journey.

Folding bikes' compatibility with other ways of getting around also means that using one offers a certain peace of mind. With the ability to 'morph' into an anonymous-looking bag of luggage, a folder isn't an obstruction to getting to your destination by another means if you can no longer just ride there.

There are folding bikes for applications from the shortest of rides to full-on touring. Folding bikes are an empowering invention, and today's crop offer even more independence and mobility. And they tuck away so neatly for storage that no cyclist should be without.

So where's the catch? To achieve portability, folders inevitably make some design compromises.

The most obvious is the smaller wheels. Rolling resistance may not be much affected on smooth surfaces given quality tyres (which are now available in almost all sizes), but as the roads get rougher, smaller wheels are definitely harder work and, unless suspended, give a harsher ride than full-size wheels. There are some full-size wheel folders (Dahon and Montague do a few models each) but they tend to be relatively heavy and bulky.

Also, with the smaller wheels, handling can be skittish unless the designer has got the geometry just right. Check that you're happy lifting a hand off the bars to indicate as you corner.

Another area where folders often compromise is in luggage capacity, though in recent years several machines have made great strides in this area. Choose the right folder and you can comfortably carry a cycle-camping load. With others, you're more or less restricted to what you can carry on your back – which may be quite sufficient for round town use.

Frame rigidity often suffers compared to a standard diamond frame. To achieve compactness, folders often end up with very long seatposts and stems, which are inherently flexy. Frame joints can also make frames feel less 'solid' and responsive than a normal bike. But again, some folding bikes hardly compromise here at all.

Finally, folders tend to be more expensive than 'normal' bikes of the same quality and weight. There's more engineering involved, with pivots and so on – and production numbers can be relatively small, reducing economies of scale. Of course there are relatively cheap folders, but then you'll find that weight and performance reflect the price.

Despite all of these factors, many cyclists find the advantages of a folder convincing enough to have one or more alongside other full-size bikes. If you can only have just one bike, you could do worse than to choose a folder.

Market overview

Performance

The first category is folders which place riding performance first. Often, these also fold very small, but require a bit of dismantling, and a little more time, to get there. They usually stick to 20" (406) wheels or larger. Bikes in this category tend not to be cheap – you're probably looking at the £800+ range – but they do offer a level of performance which should enable you to keep up with riding companions on full-size bikes. This section would definitely include models from Bike Friday, Airnimal and Moulton. Birdys and high-end Bromptons and Dahons also have a claim for inclusion here.

Compact

This is where most folders fit: bikes which collapse small or very small in seconds. But these designs are more compromised when it comes to riding performance, either by weight, more awkward riding position, lack of gearing or smaller wheels, typically 16".

That's not to say that there aren't some super bikes in this category – just that they can't necessarily claim to ride as well as your racer. The prime example of this type is the Brompton.

Simple

Where the cost and complexity of more elaborate folders isn't needed, a simple 'fold in half' job might be just the trick. These range from the heavy and flexible 'shoppers' which you can pick up for peanuts (but may not be able to lift with both hands!) to neat and relatively light machines like the Giant Halfway and the good-value and well-engineered Dahon range, or the budget Downtube.

Other

All sorts of interesting designs are available, including micro-folders, folding tandems, recumbents, and 'design'-led machines like the Airframe and the Strida. Also, for making bikes portable with few compromises, the ingenious S&S Couplings can turn any bike (or tandem) into a folder. We'll cover a few of these options later in this chapter.

Where to find out about and try them

It really is an extremely good idea to try before you buy, and in any case to do some research. Some of the best sources for detailed folding bike info are:

» *A to B Magazine:* Specialising in folding and electric bikes, *A to B* comes out bimonthly and, for the modest cost of £12 in the UK, I recommend a subscription. It often contains reviews of folders – also, check out their website for a listing of UK folder prices and brief recommendations. Tel 01963 351 649 or see www.atob.org.uk

» *Folding Society News:* This enthusiast website is a great resource if you're after a folder. It contains links to manufacturers' websites, to user groups and mailing lists, and also contains a good number of reader-submitted reviews. See: www.foldsoc.org.uk

» Manufacturers all produce leaflets and printed information about their products – just ask.

» Visit specialist dealers – see the list at the end of this chapter. They'll often have a selection of models for you to try.

Folding bikes don't come up often secondhand – and when they do, they tend to get snapped up fast! Good places to look include the free small ads at our Velo Vision website (www.velovision.com), and small ads in *A to B* and the CTC magazine *Cycle*. And do keep an eye on the small ads in your local paper, and the internet equivalents such as Gumtree.

Folding bikes

Commuting folders

For daily use on sometimes-crowded trains, followed by urban riding. Really it's hard to recommend anything but a Brompton. It still has the smallest and neatest fold without overly compromising the ride. But some alternatives have more to offer for longer rides, or trump the Brompton in speed of folding. These include the Mezzo, Birdy and Bike Friday Tikit models.

Brompton

Booming popularity of folding bikes in London has led to Brompton's ever-expanding factory working flat out for pretty much the last decade keeping up with demand – and not without reason. It's been the folding bike benchmark for decades.

Key to the attraction is the folding mechanism, which results in a tidy bundle with the oily bits inside, all securely held together so that it can be carried with confidence. Almost uniquely, it also stands up securely at every stage of the folding process, much reducing the co-ordination required. Recent revisions have left the Brompton with a ride which is bordering on excellent: the steering geometry is fine, and the rear suspension offers a smooth ride despite the small, high-pressure tyres. My only real quibbles are the brakes and the gears. Braking is OK verging on mediocre, mainly thanks to an idiosyncratic own-brand brake lever design (easily changed if it bothers you). The gearing is limited by the bike's very narrow rear triangle, which limits the standard options available: you can't fit a normal hub gear or derailleur system in. Brompton's solutions are adequate for town use, but struggle in the hills or if you take the bike on tour.

The Brompton model range has expanded and modernised in recent years, with optional titanium parts, colourful paintwork and a choice of handlebar designs now on offer. Prices range from around £520 to well over £1000, with higher price bringing you more accessories, lighter components and wider gear range. Bromptons do hold their value well,

and second-hand ones are usually quickly snapped up.

This brings us to one last possible problem: actually getting hold of one. Over the last year or two waiting lists have been measured in months, and other brands have perhaps profited from this lack of immediate availability. Some dealers do get stocks in occasionally, though, so try ringing round!

Brompton: Tel 020 8232 8484 or see www.bromptonbicycle.com

Mezzo

The Mezzo is another UK-made folder, and Brompton rival, and it does have a number of points in its favour. The folded package isn't as small or as neat, but it does use clever quick-release and self-locking which make the folding action quick and satisfying. It does without suspension, but this gives it a rigid, sporty ride, and most standard drivetrain options can be fitted. Luggage capacity is limited as yet, but it does come fitted with mudguards.

There are currently three versions: the i4 (around £595) uses the Shimano 4-speed hub, a favourite of mine for utility use and with great under-load shifting, if a bit limited in range. The d9 (£625) uses 9-speed Shimano Capreo derailleur gearing. Just launched is a new 10-speed derailleur model, the d10, using a more curvaceous frame design, and expected to be higher up the price scale than the earlier models.

Mezzo: Tel 01424 753 566 or see www.mezzobikes.com

Birdy

For many years the main Brompton alternative, the Birdy is an aluminium-framed, full-suspension machine which folds fairly fast to around Brompton-and-a-half sort of size. It has always targeted the ride and performance

more than the Brompton, and the lightweight, rigid frame is, I find, simply more enjoyable to ride, especially if you're a strong rider. Very lightweight models are available (at a price) as are well-equipped tourers. These make capable all-rounders, and the size/performance mix is just about right for weekends away by train – it tucks away behind train seats, but is good enough for a decent day-ride too, even in the hills.

Birdy have several UK dealers, and prices range from around £1000 to £2000. See www.r-m.de for a dealer list.

Bike Friday Tikit

If the Mezzo takes the Brompton and makes the fold faster, but bigger, then the Bike Friday Tikit takes it one step further. With an ingenious design

which links the various folding joints together via cables, the fold is near-instant: there's video online of a rider folding the bike in the same motion as he dismounts and walks off (http://tinyurl.com/5ve8x9).

The result, though, is a rather long, thin folded package, two to three times the bulk of a Brompton (the larger frame sizes are not surprisingly larger when folded, too). But it rolls along easily on its front wheel even when folded, much easier than lifting it. A bag on the front carrier can stay in place, too. Another neat feature is the fabric cover, built in to fold away on the main frame.

The ride is very good: the relatively long wheelbase helps smooth out the bumps, and a standard drivetrain lets you specify as many gears as you require. V-brakes provide good stopping, and folding carrier racks can take two full panniers at the back. Only the stem had a little too much flex on the early version I tried.

Available via several UK dealers, or see www.bikefriday.com

Urban runabout folders

A new genre seems to be developing for apartment-dwelling urbanites who want a compact, stylish bike on which to get around and run errands, and which can be stowed away flat against a wall or under the stairs. Clearly many bikes could suit, but machines aimed at this niche include the flat-barred version of the Bridgestone Moulton, the Airnimal Joey, Dahon's Hon Solo and Mike Burrows' single-speed 2D.

Bridgestone Moulton: Lovely little town bike, almost too nice for the job though at £1225. Very light, with very responsive suspension. Separates simply into two rather large halves. Alex Moulton Bicycles: Tel 01225 865895 or see www. alexmoulton.co.uk

Airnimal Joey: Fast-riding, good-looking machine and not too pricey at £695. Quick-release to fold handlebars flat, and various stages of (not super fast) folding right down to suitcase size. See www.airnimal.eu

Dahon Hon Solo: Lovely limited edition folder with wood and leather trim, swept-back bars and custom paintwork. Not out of reach either at around £700 in the UK, but as the name suggests you'll have to enjoy the minimalism of singlespeed riding. If you can't find one any more,

check out Dahon's website for details of their latest 'specials' – often very nice bikes. www.dahon.com

Burrows 2D: Carbon-fibre monostay, single-speed runabout with totally enclosed drive and unique designer appeal. Handles nicely, could be just the job if you want a stylish bike that's a bit

different, but not for the weak of wallet at £1500. Flattens, but does not fold. Burrows Engineering: Tel 01603 721 700.

'Road bike' folders

Beloved of jet-set racing cyclists who want a bike with them for fast rides or training without the hassle and risk of transporting a full-sized machine by air. Airnimal's Chameleon, the Bike Friday models and the Pacific Reach are front-runners here.

Bike Friday: UK importers Avon Valley Cyclery bring in a wide range of these USA-made folding bikes. The entry-level model in their 'road' range, the Pocket Pilot, starts at 'just' £695. Models go up to over £2000, with the titanium beam-suspended Air Friday. Tandems and tourers available too. Bike Fridays are known for a rigid and responsive ride, and many options for handlebars, luggage etc. See www.bikefriday.com, and in the UK contact Avon Valley Cyclery: www.foldingbikes.co.uk

Airnimal Chameleon: The Chameleon is the 'performance travel' model in the range and starts at around £1000. With a bit of work, it packs down very small (hand-luggage size, minus the wheels) and it also has an excellent ride, with a hardish elastomer just to take out the harshness of the 24" wheels. Plenty of racks, mudguards etc. are also available. Tel 01223 523973 or see www.airnimal. eu

Pacific Reach: Made under their own name by Taiwan's Pacific Cycles, who make many of the other folding bikes we've listed, this is a good-value fast folder with smooth suspension and a unique look. Available in the UK from £599 from Airnimal: www.airnimal.eu.

Off-road folders

The Airnimal Rhino and Dahon's 26" wheel range are the main options here, along with the 'Paratrooper' from Montague. Some Bike Fridays are also off-roaders, although their suspension doesn't seem quite as 'serious' as the Rhino's. Clearly for the most extreme off-roading you'll always want the bigger wheels, but for rough road or track use the smaller-wheeled machines can have very acceptable performance.

Airnimal Rhino: With 20" wheels and air shock suspension at the back, the Rhino is apparently also popular for smoothing rides on potholed urban commutes or back-roads tours where its portability is also essential. Starts at around £1375.

Montague Paratrooper: This military-styled 26"-wheeled folder is certainly a contender if you need a car-boot friendly fold and off-road capability. At around £495 you do get some fairly basic components on the folding frame, and fitting effective mudguards and carrying racks is somewhat tricky. But it looks great and folds very easily. Tel 01730 711140 or see www.montague-uk.com

Dahon Flo: this is top of Dahon's 26" wheeled range, and the only real 'mountain bike' in there — the rest (starting at £330 or so) are more for urban or leisure use. The 10.2 kg, £1499 Flo is separable rather than folding, using a very unobtrusive system.

Touring folders

Folding bikes make excellent tourers, offering versatility and convenience not just for transport, but also for overnight: they'll often be able to sleep in a room or tent with you rather than less securely outside or in a hotel 'lock-up'. But they're usually not designed to carry as much luggage as a conventional touring bike. So the options are limited to folders with good luggage capacity, and, preferably, a wide range of gears. Here's a quick run-down of the options from the various manufacturers:

» Bike Friday: Well proven as tourers, with plenty of luggage options. Their full-on tourers are not cheap – it's £1100 or more for a 'New World Tourist' model with wide-ratio transmission.

» Airnimal: The availability of spares for the 24" wheel size may be a concern in remote areas, but otherwise the Chameleon or a Joey with racks added would make a good tourer.

» Birdy: Latest models have good luggage carrying capacity front and rear, (as pictured), and if you can afford the Touring model (with Shimano 3x7 gears, around £1100+) or even the Rohloff-equipped Birdy Grey (£1900-odd) you'll get a good range of gears too. Again, with 18" (355) wheels, there are possible tyre availability concerns, but carrying a spare isn't such a big deal.

» Moulton: separables, not folders of

course, as they split in two rather than fold as such. But the Moulton's suspended ride comfort does make it attractive as a tourer, though it's also somewhat limited by the narrow tyre clearances and luggage options. Perhaps the Pashley-made Moulton APBs (from £700ish, or around £850 with wide-range gears) are a more sensible choice than the beautiful but pricey Alex Moulton versions. Tel 01789 292 263 or see www.pashley.co.uk

» And finally there's the Dahon Cadenza, with full-sized wheels and a very

discreet folding mechanism. The 'normal' looks and 26" wheels make it a good choice for touring in developing countries where the attention a smaller-wheeled bike attracts can be overwhelming. The frame is also super-versatile, accommodating all sorts of brakes, with an eccentric bottom bracket for hub gears, and with mounts for luggage. At around £580 in the UK it's a solid base for a touring bike, and comes with some good components already fitted. Available via the many Dahon dealers, or see www.dahon.com

Occasional use folders

A good number of folding bikes are bought for weekend use, to be carried in the boot of a car to somewhere nice for a round-trip day-ride. For this sort of use the super-costly models are often ruled out (though they'd do the job superbly) and so a Dahon is probably the first to spring to mind – great value and good machines, and widely available. Another one to check out is the Downtube, a good-value US brand with a UK distributor. All of these are fold-in-the-middle designs, considerably bigger than the Brompton but still easily swallowed by most car boots. Also worth a look, but a bit more pricey, is the Giant Halfway.

Dahon: Unless space is at a premium, or you're a very tiny rider, a 20"-wheeled Dahon Boardwalk at around £280 is a good bike. If you can stretch to £330 or so you get the much nicer Vitesse D7, with aluminium frame. There are plenty of even more capable and lighter Dahons at higher prices, well worth a look. Dealers can be found via www.dahon.co.uk

Downtube: With prices from just £200, you might expect bargain-basement performance. But it's actually not a bad bike: components are

The Downtube folding bike

mostly pretty decent, and the aluminium frame is lightweight and solid. Suspension versions are also available, along with a 'mini' model with 16" rather than 20" wheels (available with Sturmey 8-speed hub gears. for £300). Hinges are a bit ugly but do the job. Lacking rather in luggage options, but overall, hard to beat for the money. See www.downtube.com or, in the UK, contact www.velochocolate.co.uk.

Giant Halfway: At around £400, it's a nice rigid ride, and in a touch of Burrows design class, the 20" wheels are supported one-sided for easy puncture-fixing. Luggage capacity is lacking, limiting it to short trips. From Giant dealers everywhere.

Boaty folders

There's a little niche among boat-owners for corrosion-resistant folders with style for forays on-shore: great performance is less of a priority than low maintenance. The Strida fits in here, along with some stainless-steel folders by Italian manufacturer di Blasi. I must admit I'm surprised that these yacht owners don't all just buy Bromptons, with space at such a premium on board, and money presumably not terribly tight. Surely they wouldn't corrode all that fast?

Folders on public transport

Train

In Britain at least, folding bikes are increasingly the only hassle-free option when it comes to combining trains with cycling. A few hints from my experience:

» If at all possible get a bag for your folder. When luggage space is tight, damaging other passengers' luggage is then less of a concern. It also makes the bike slightly less obvious to potential thieves.

» Often, on long journeys where I may nod off, I'll lock the bike to the luggage rack. Or, see if it'll go between the seat backs – it seems more secure there. A thinnish, flexible cable lock is sufficient, just to stop someone grabbing it as they get off. Folding bikes have been stolen from trains, so be wary.

» Often when travelling with a folder it's easier if you don't have to remove all of your lights, luggage etc. and actually fold it. So, if it's free and easily done, I'll just book a bike place in the luggage van and wheel the bike on and off intact, keeping the folding 'in reserve' for emergencies.

» Consider how you'll carry folded bike and luggage. If you have a lot of luggage and a shortish cycle leg of the journey, then a big rucksack can work well: it's easy to walk with and leaves both hands free for carrying the folded bike. Certainly try to avoid having lots of little bags to carry – or perhaps strap them together so they're more easily managed. Most quality panniers, when bought in pairs, will include a suitable strap so they can be linked together.

Taxi

Again, a lightweight bag to enclose the bike should help avoid hassle from cabbies worried about dirt or scratches. With a folding bike, calling a taxi is an easy way to get yourself out of trouble if you're stuck.

Bus

Local buses are tricky; there's often very limited luggage space, and what there is can be hard to lift your bike into. And there's usually no room to leave the bike in the aisles without causing an obstruction. A Brompton could fit on your lap I suppose...

Coaches are a different matter: there's a cavernous hold down below: the difficult bit can be to persuade the driver. Once again, get that fabric cover, and make sure there aren't obvious metal bits poking out to damage either the vehicle or others' luggage.

Air travel

It's a perennial problem for full-sized and folding bike riders alike: how do you keep the bike safe from the notorious baggage-handlers, but not end up encumbered with a vast hard-shell box or suitcase at the other end? You could just package the bike up well at home, then trust you can scavenge packaging for the trip back. Or, if you can arrange it without excessive cost, send on your suitcase to your departure point and have it held in storage.

With folding bikes, you may as well make use of their smaller folded size and just box them up. If you've saved the original box the bike came in so much the better — if not, ask the dealer who supplied it. Chances are they'll have one spare.

Find out more

Specialist dealers

Try the following dealers to see a good selection of models in one visit. It's well worth buying from a local dealer if possible – many folding bikes do have some manufacturer-specific intricacies when it comes to servicing. Check the websites, too – they often offer good advice and info.

» Avon Valley Cycles in Bath: 01225 442 442 or www.foldingbikes.co.uk

» Bicycle Doctor in Manchester: 0161 224 1303 or www.bicycledoctor.co.uk

» Bikefix in London: Tel 020 7405 1218 or www.bikefix.co.uk

» Biketrax in Edinburgh: 0131 228 6633 or www.biketrax.co.uk

» Cycle Heaven in York: 01904 636578 or www.cycle-heaven.co.uk

» Cycle-Ops in Tunbridge, Kent: 01732 500 533 or www.cycle-ops.co.uk

» Kinetics in Glasgow: 0141 942 2552 or www.kbikes.co.uk

» Norman Fay Cycles in South Shields (Newcastle/Gateshead): 0191 456 1055 or www.normanfaycycles.co.uk

» Spa Cycles in Harrogate: 01423 887 003 or www.spacycles.co.uk

Folding bike-specific events are relatively rare: some UK 'Origami' folder rides are publicised via the Folding Society website www.foldsoc.org.uk, and there's the 'Round-Up' event in Philadelphia, USA in early June each year: see www.trophybikes.com. The German user clubs for Birdy (www.birdy-freunde.de) and Brompton (www.bromptonauten.de) are quite active and have regular rides and meetings. Brompton, Birdy and Bike Friday also operate their own events on occasion: see their websites for details.

Also worth a mention

Airframe: aluminium folder with a somewhat flexy frame – which some say gives it a 'responsive' ride. Light, but doesn't fold super-small, and also limited gear range and luggage capacity. See www.airframebike.com or Tel 01582 609988

Pacific Carry-Me: Ultra-small, super-light microfolder which is surprisingly capable. Incomparably better than the Sinclair A-Bike! Sub 8 kg, single-speed or with Schlumpf two-speed gearing. Available in the UK from Airnimal: Tel 01954 782 020 or see www.pacific-products.co.uk

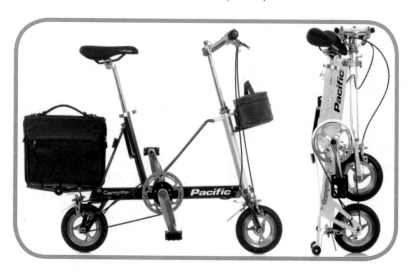

Mobiky Genius: (right) A very clever fold and a surprisingly rigid frame make this £499 bike much more capable than you'd expect from the tiny

wheels, but it's let down by its weight. A larger-wheeled version is in the works as we go to press. UK importers are CycleCentric: www.cyclecentric. co.uk.

Strida: These distinctively triangular bikes take a little getting used to, but for some they are a lightweight, distinctive and clean (they use a belt drive) alternative. Also affordable, from £380 or so in the UK. Single speed limits it to short hops. The new Strida5 version looks particularly nice, with spoked wheels and disk brakes. See www.strida.com or Tel 0121 681 0964.

Koga Founder-S: Solid-looking folder with nice styling and full suspension from Koga in the Netherlands. Now available through dealers in the UK, but pricey at £1000+. See www.koga. com for a dealer list.

S&S couplings: These let you 'split' any bike frame tube, then reassemble without losing stiffness or adding much weight. This allows even tandems to fit in suitcases. Fitted by framebuilders or manufacturers, either as original equipment or as a retro-fit to an existing (steel tubed) frame. Not a cheap option (for most solo bikes, anything up to £500 extra, and more for tandems), but effective and well proven. Available in various sizes so

most tandems and recumbents can also be fitted with them. See www.sandsmachine.com for details.

Family cycling

Family cycling usually means cycling with children, and in this section we'll be looking at the special challenges and opportunities this poses. We'll also examine in some detail the related area of tandem cycling, with or without children.

Most children want to cycle, given half a chance. Getting a first bicycle and learning to ride it is a rite of passage in many families, even in today's world where electronic amusements seem to be overtaking mechanical ones. Even where the parents aren't regular cyclists, children will often have a bike as a toy in their early years.

Alas, for many children it's never taken any further, and there's no attempt to show that cycling can move from passing amusement to a useful way to get around.

Relatively few move from the back garden, the pavement and the local park onto the roads. It's a shame, if only because they're missing out on cycling skills that could well come in handy in later life – perhaps as a teenager desperate for independent mobility.

For parents who are cyclists, the question is rather different: going places by bike is a given, and it's more a case of how best to take the children with you in comfort and safety, with the child's introduction to cycling following on as a natural progression.

First we'll take a look at some of the equipment available to make family cycling easier and safer, then we'll concentrate on advice about how to ride with children – and how to teach them to ride themselves.

Why family cycling?

Cycling with children is often hard to explain to non-cyclists, especially if you go beyond leisure rides on sunny weekends. It's as if you're somehow making your hapless offspring suffer for your own odd obsession.

Yet nothing could be further from the truth. Done right, cycling is safe, great fun and an enjoyable way for children to get around, at more or less any age and in more or less any weather. It's health-enhancing of course, but also has some less easily-definable benefits. Getting places on a bike (once you've outgrown a trailer) as an active contributor to motion, rather than as a passive passenger in the back seat of a car, is, in that dread phrase, character-building.

Finally, of course, cycling is very often the fastest and most efficient form of transport. Cruise past the child-chauffeuring parents queuing in the school run traffic jams, and drop your child off at the gates. Just as for solo cycling, the bike allows families to filter through the clogged arteries of urban life.

How far it's possible to conduct your family's activities by bike will depend on where you live and the environment you inhabit. But with the right knowledge, equipment and attitude it's amazing what can be done enjoyably and safely.

Money matters

Often when advising friends and family on family cycling options all goes well until the price of a particular bike or accessory is mentioned. HOW much?

Family budgets are often tight, so some of the more expensive options we discuss will be simply unaffordable for many. Or so it seems... it's all a question of priorities. Here is not the place to go into the potential savings of going car-free, but if cycling is your main form of transport then budget accordingly. Buy well and the equipment will be safe, durable, lightweight and a pleasure to use. You'll have forgotten the cost before long, but the breeze in your hair and the enjoyment will last for years.

There's also a nice surprise waiting. The resale value of specialist family cycling gear is extremely good – a quality used child trailer might only lose 25% of its value in a couple of years. Family tandems and the like are sought-after and will usually sell easily second-hand. The money can then be re-invested on the next step on the child-carrying ladder.

Age range overview

There are cycling solutions to transport children from just a few weeks old through to adulthood: we'll cover these in detail later. Here's how the sequence goes as your child grows older:

Babies:	Car seats in trailers, or the Babybike
Toddlers:	Trailers or childseats
2-5:	Toy trikes, scooters, Like-a-Bike
4-10ish	Trailerbikes, child's bikes
5-8ish	Tandem with kiddycranks, child's bikes
7-12ish	Childback tandems, child's bikes
12+	Time for their own bike, or continue on the tandem.

Teaching children to ride

There are several different approaches to teaching children to ride.

The 'traditional' way is to use training wheels, which essentially turn a child's bike into a tricycle. The idea is that you then gradually raise them, forcing the child to balance or pedal leaned right over. This is my least favourite method: trikes and bikes have completely different dynamics, so it's odd to train on one in an attempt to learn the other.

If you're not convinced, try riding an upright trike! If you've developed your skills on two wheels, a tricycle will be an unnerving experience to say the least. It's as bad the other way round.

Also, a certain speed is really needed to balance a two-wheeler, and training wheels in contact with the ground add considerable resistance, the last thing a young cyclist needs, especially if they're already on a heavy bike with cheap bearings. And they also make it more or less impossible to practice on grass, a much more forgiving surface than tarmac for the inevitable tumbles.

Another way is to walk or run alongside the child, holding him or her up with a hand on the shoulder as they get the hang of steering. This is a good method – if you're pushing they won't have to pedal to keep up speed, and can concentrate on steering and balance. But it can be exhausting...

The third way is generally regarded as the best, and separates the skills of balancing and pedalling. It requires either a child's bicycle with pedals removed, or a purpose-built scooter such as the Like-a-bike or one of its many imitators.

With no pedals to get in the way, the child can easily get both feet on the floor, a great reassurance. Scooting along is almost as easy as walking, and as the speed builds up the child will be balancing before they know it. The least hint of a downhill will have them going 'wheeee' and lifting both feet – bingo, they're balanced!

A scooter is definitely superior to a small bike here: it'll be useful from an earlier age, much lighter, and it'll usually also be safer without spoked wheels or transmission to create possible hazards. There are versions with fattish tyres which will be great for learning outside on grass, or solid-tyred models for indoor or hard standing use.

Tot transport

Until children are quite a bit older, they'll need to be transported by stronger and older leg-power. This can cover both utility cycling and longer leisure rides and outings.

Fortunately the utility journeys that most parents need to make on a regular basis by bike are short – otherwise they wouldn't be practical by bike, with or without children. A ten or fifteen minute bike ride to school, shopping or to visit friends or relatives is quite manageable by childseat or trailer. A trailer is probably the better option for year-round use: not only is it safer to load up (with space for other items too) but it gives protection from rain, sun and cold air. Toys and other amusements can be in there with the child for entertainment too. Many children apparently fall asleep in child trailers…

One problem with trailers is the bulk, and although most good models will fold flat for storage, it's not something you'd want to do at the start of finish of every journey, simultaneously trying to keep your offspring under control. Childseats have a real advantage here – usually they can just be left on the bike. Whether the bulky trailers issue is really a problem will depend on the destination and your facilities at home. It's usually no problem leaving a trailer outside a supermarket or school.

A further option is a dedicated child and load-carrying vehicle, usually a tricycle. As well as the Nihola, Christiania and Kangaroo models from Denmark, there's also the Bakfiets two-wheeler from the Netherlands. All offer superb stability and road presence, and come equipped with rain and sun canopies, just like most child trailers.

Such vehicles, and quality child trailers, have excellent resale value once they're outgrown. Or ditch the child-carrying bits and just employ them as load-carriers.

Outings

Children, quite naturally, have rather different tastes from committed cyclists when it comes to days out. For a leisure cyclist the journey itself, and the pleasure of bowling along, is its own reward. A child may also appreciate that pleasure – but only for a little while, and if they're a passive passenger, even less.

Variety is the thing. Plenty of stops, plenty of interest. This doesn't necessarily mean a carefully-plotted course between tourist attractions: instead let the child him or herself point out what's fun, and go with it. See a horse in a field? Stop and say hello! Ducks on a village pond? Spooky graveyard of a church? Explore, if you dare…

Another great way to add fun and variety is to go out with other families – if you can organise it! That gives all of the children companions to play with, a chance to compare notes, and also reassurance that being out and about by bike is a perfectly normal activity that other people do, too.

Travelling as a couple with a child in the trailer, a tandem is a tempting option. It means both riders share the work of towing the trailer, and it's a compact unit on the road. A tandem is also a great towing vehicle, with superior brakes well up to stopping the trailer's extra weight, and no chance of jack-knifing under heavy braking.

On the other hand, if the stronger rider tows the trailer behind a solo bike, the other parent can ride alongside or behind the trailer to talk to the child. It also feels very safe with the child's trailer sandwiched between the two adult riders.

If you have a car, take the scooter or bike with you on outings. If you're going somewhere towing a bike trailer, strap or stow the child's own bike or scooter on board too, so that they can enjoy a blast around themselves when you stop. They'll love a chance to pedal and explore for themselves after being cooped up for the journey.

Adult-assisted pedalling

As the child gets a little older, say four upwards, it's definitely a good idea to involve them in the pedalling. At this stage they will already have got the hang of balance and pedalling via the scooter/child's bike methods as above, but they're not old enough to take solo responsibility for mixing with traffic on the roads.

Instead, they can help you pedal! You get a little help, and they'll also gain in a number of ways. Pedalling makes every journey a team effort: they can be proud of their contribution, as they've got you there just as much as the parent. The effort of pedalling also removes a constant worry with trailer towing or child seats – children getting too cold. The only thing to watch is if a young pedaller gets sleepy – you can't really nod off perched on a saddle as you can in a seat. So especially at first, the trips need to be kept short.

Technically, there are several possibilities at this stage, and as ever your particular circumstances, budget and taste will decide:

» A childback tandem is probably the ideal vehicle: a tandem with a very small frame at the back for the child pedaller. This offers a lovely stable ride, is relatively compact and, if your adult rear rider is short, may well suit two adults too. It's easy for the child to get on and off independently, which  is a nice bonus. But it can be a big investment to make for a few years, though you'll get most of it back when you sell.

» Fit a normal tandem with kiddy-cranks. There are an extra pair of cranks fitted to the stoker's seatpost and linked to the main drive by a short extra chain. The child is rather high up for getting on and off, but on the road it's perfectly stable. There's an additional bonus if the child's kiddicrank is fitted with a freewheel so that they can stop pedalling if they get tired. Normally on a tandem the pedals are linked, so both partners are forced to pedal at the same pace. Available from most tandem specialist dealers — see later in this chapter.

» Use a trailerbike, also known as a tag-a-long. This gives the child rather

more independence, with their own set of gears and proper handlebars, and provides the freewheel function. I still can't recommend anything except the Burley Piccolo or the relaunched Islabikes trailerbike. Most of the other brands I've seen

– including some well-known names – seem woefully inadequate in the engineering of the pivot. Tracking and stability is also much better on the Piccolo and Islabikes models which have the pivot directly over the rear wheel on a reinforced carrier rack, rather than attached high up on the seatpost.

»   There have been various designs of 'towing link' over the years, designed to lift the front wheel of a child's own bike off the ground and trail it

along behind an adult bike, similar to a trailerbike. A very few have been well engineered and safe. Some have been dire. Be wary. That said, it's a neat solution, and allows the child to explore solo if you stop off at a park or similar.

»   If you ride recumbent, your child will want to too! The only commercially-available option is the Hase Trets two-wheeled trailerbike, expensive but excellent.

Riding with an adult in this way, even for short utility rides, is a great way

for a child to pick up on skills almost unconsciously, and all with the adult taking care of safety in traffic. You can keep up a commentary rather like one of those road safety videos, identifying hazards. Involve your child rear rider in signalling. Changing gear will become second nature, so it's not a distraction later. And the subtleties of speed control, road positioning and negotiating with traffic will all soak in even if it's a bit early to start teaching this directly. Finally, they'll note how you always lock the bike up when parking it – a valuable lesson for later life.

Riding solo

After some time assisting an adult, children will be itching to ride on their own. Naturally you'll have to cut back the distances again, and also choose routes with some care. Build up gradually, from coping with other cyclists on a railway path, perhaps, to quiet, wide roads on a Sunday morning before venturing into more difficult traffic conditions as you judge the child's capabilities growing.

As in any group ride, it's best if the weaker rider goes first – so the child in front, with an adult behind. This way the child won't ever despair of falling behind, and both riders get a view forwards. The adult can move out protectively to ensure passing cars give space, or ride alongside if it's safe to chat.

Cycling with a novice of any age can certainly be a nerve-wracking experience, especially if you're a practiced cyclist who knows just what not to do! There's just too much to say, too much distilled experience to pass over. Attempting to say it all at once just doesn't work, and can end up sounding as if you're telling the rider they're doing it all wrong... not much fun for either of you. Better to keep relaxed – after all, many cyclists bumble along quite happily without much clue at all about cycling in traffic, and most of the time no harm ensues. Try not to worry, and stay positive!

Leisure riding

Cycling as a family – or several families out together – inevitably involves catering for riders of differing abilities. We've already discussed how to keep children's interest by frequent, often impromptu stops (and food and drink can be good excuses for further breaks), but if you have a choice of routes you can build in some further little tricks:

For obvious reasons, go out against the wind, and back with it. Out uphill, back downhill.

If your route can't avoid hills altogether, tackle the long gradual hills on the way out if you can, and keep the short steep ones for the way back. It's less draining to walk up a few quick hills than it is to slog endlessly upwards.

It's more relaxing to ride with traffic if you're going fast, preferably downhill or with a tailwind. So if you do have to take in busy roads, check the contours and try to make that stretch gravity-assisted.

Child commuting

In the UK, more and more schools (with some shameful exceptions) are encouraging pupils to arrive by bike. Sustrans operate an excellent Safe Routes to Schools programme, improving infrastructure and parking as well as educating both school staff and pupils. And cycle training is rolling out nationwide, so that ever more children are formally being taught the basic of riding. The better schemes cover cycling in traffic skills, too.

Many parents will cycle with their children to school, but a few innovative schemes have been set up with 'cycling buses' where a parent or teacher leads a group of cycling children, picking up riders en route. Contact Sustrans (Tel 0845 113 00 65 or see www.sustrans.org.uk) or the CTC (Tel 0870 873 0060 or see www.ctc.org.uk) for hints about setting one up yourself.

But there's some way yet to go until we reach the level of child cycling in mainland Europe. I remember cycling through the outskirts of Amsterdam once, seeing whole classes of schoolchildren cycling along, presumably between schools or on outings. And the after-school bicycle rush had to be seen to be believed.

If your child is commuting by bike, to school or elsewhere, then a reliable bike will save you time and money. Hub gears, hub dynamos and sensor lighting might be going a bit far, but why not? If lights are always on the bike then they'll never forget them. Flashing pedals from Pedalite or Ledal are another good safety idea. Bicycle maintenance and decoration is another great opportunity to involve children, and to encourage them to take responsibility for their own vehicle's safety. Unlike many of the electronic gadgets around today, cycles can be repaired and fine-tuned with simple tools, a satisfying experience at any age.

Security can be an issue for children's bikes, as they're often not too punctilious about locking them up, not to mention losing the keys. A combination lock can help with the keys at least…

Incidentally there is plenty of support available should a child wish to try their hand (or legs) at cycle sport. Ask at your local cycle club, or contact British Cycling on 0870 871 2000 or see www.britishcycling.org.uk

There are also many excellent resources for disabled children who would like to cycle, and we'll refer to some in a later chapter of this book.

Family cycling – equipment

Car seats and the Babybike

Most people don't know that babies of just a few months old can be carried safely and comfortably by bike. What you need is a car seat: these have been extensively tested and developed for carrying really young 'uns.

They're just as effective mounted in a car trailer or on the bike as they are on the back seat of a car.

Car childseats come with a good harness, and are designed to support the infant fully. They're padded against vibration and warm. Often they are fitted with a carrying handle so that they can also be used to transport the child off the bike.

Several trailer manufacturers offer kits to fit child seats securely into their trailers. Seats can also be mounted effectively and safely onto various load-carrying machines including the Christiania, Nihola and 8-Freight.

Although I have reservations about two-wheelers and childseats (see later) one product which deserves special mention is the BabyBike. It's a suspended attachment system for a car childseat which fits onto a standard rear rack (get a strong one!). The car seat is fitted via a quick-release system into a reclined position which allows children as young as just a few months old to sleep comfortably with full neck support. A 'tent' cover adds rain and wind protection.

The Babybike website (www.babybike.com) is frankly dire. But I've yet to hear of an owner who hasn't sung the actual product's praises. To get hold of one, you have to order direct from the manufacturer in the Netherlands: Tel +31 35 695 1908 or email babybike@tip.nl

Childseats

Perhaps it's too-long exposure to the wide and wonderful world of specialist bikes and trikes, but I must admit that I cringe when I see a child seat on a two-wheeled bicycle. Yet surely thousands of parents can't be wrong?

Clearly, sticking a seat on the back rack of a normal bike is the cheapest and simplest method of child-carrying, and also the most compact and convenient for storage. As such I shouldn't really knock it. Yet the simple fact is that a two-wheeler is not an easy or stable platform onto which to load a child. It can fall over.

Luckily, most modern childseats are designed with an element of 'roll-cage' type protection, and the manufacturers recommend that the passenger wears a helmet. This is at best a partial solution.

Better, if you can possibly arrange it, is to do your child-carrying on three wheels or consider a trailer. If not, at least get a solid two-leg stand to make loading safer.

As to the seats themselves, the rear-rack type are much of a muchness. The weight limit for most is around 18 kg, or 40 lb, and this should not be exceeded. You get what you pay for in terms of quality: a good seat will have a robust mounting and a comfortable, easily adjusted and childproof harness. It's essential that the child's feet are kept well away from spokes. Removable, washable upholstery is also a good idea, as is the option of using normal panniers with the seat.

Only a few of these seats recline so as to provide any significant support for the neck of a sleeping child. If a child does drop off to sleep and the head lolls off to one side it's easy for damage to be done. A neck cushion may help a bit but it's not a good solution.

A potentially better system is a seat which fits in front of the rider, so the child sits between your arms. This is a reassuring position for both child and parent – plus the child gets a good view! The main UK brand for this type is currently the Weeride (www.weerideuk.co.uk), retailing at around £60. Many advantages are claimed, including a better view for the passenger, easy conversation and observation, and improved stability. You can also use the rear rack for luggage. It thoughtfully provides a cushioned front rest onto which a sleepy child can lean and sleep. Users report that it pretty much lives up to its claims – with the significant proviso that it requires a distinctly knees-out pedalling action which can be uncomfortable over longer rides.

It attaches to almost any bike via a beam fitted between seatpost and head tube. Extra beams are available, so the seat can be fitted in seconds to either parents' bike.

Trailers

If there's one really competitive area of the family cycling market it's trailers. With some excellent machines coming from Europe, Canada, the USA and elsewhere there's a huge choice – from bargain basement models in supermarkets to sophisticated, suspended vehicles.

Contrary to the belief of many motorists, a child in a trailer is considerably safer than one in a childseat. Not only is the 'falling over' problem avoided, but trailers offer considerable all-round protection for a child passenger. Extensive research in Germany has shown that even in impacts with cars, trailers fare very well – sliding, rather than crushing. And in any case, a trailer is a very visible thing on the road, and usually tends to engender respect from drivers.

Trailers have a number of other advantages. The child has their own 'territory' inside the trailer, and can be fully kitted out with toys, drinks and the like. There's usually extra space for shopping etc if needed. Also, the 'tent' of the trailer offers insulation against cold winds, road grit and rain. It can be so comfortable that some parents resort to taking their offspring for a trailer ride last thing at night, just to get the little monsters to fall asleep!

Many trailers will accommodate two children, and once it starts to get crowded and the kids move on to other solutions the trailer will still be a useful load-carrier (or even dog-carrier!).

Burley, Chariot, Leggero and Weber all make splendid trailers, as do others. I'd strongly suggest going to a specialist trailer dealer such as Bikesandtrailers or D-Tek to really discover the differences and features of the various models, and why it's worth paying a bit more for a good one rather than a supermarket special. This might include hitch quality, versatility and design, wheel and bearing quality, weight (steel or aluminium...) and ease of use and comfort of harness and seat. Many trailers fold down flat for storage. Some have suspension for a more stable and comfortable ride, and some even incorporate automatic braking systems for the trailer wheels to minimise 'shunting'.

The Burley Dee trailer looks like an extremely attractive option, at a retail price of around £200. That's half the price of their benchmark D'Lite model, long regarded as among the best around. See www.burley.com. They have distributors all over.

Scooters

A scooter without pedals can be an ideal way to teach the essentials of balance from a young age. There are now several versions of the Like-a-Bike, covering on and off road use, and it's still perhaps the best of the bunch. Like-a-bike UK: Tel 01937 530303 or see www.likeabike.co.uk

It does have its imitators now, and some are very good too. Islabikes have a scooter bike, the Rothan, which is well made and light.

The Rennrad from Germany is a clever scooter to which pedals can be added later. Tel +49 8093 90360 or see www.moving-children.de.

Children's bikes

Children love independent mobility and from an early age will enjoy play on toy tricycles, tiny bikes and scooters. As they get a bit older they'll probably still need to use a trailerbike or the like for being transported on busy roads, but will also look to getting their own bike. Unfortunately children's bikes tend to be cheap and very heavy: the consequence of parents not wanting to spend too much on something soon to be outgrown, and of manufacturers designing in healthy safety margins against inevitable abuse.

So exercise caution about cheap children's bikes from mass market outlets. Avoid suspension, as it just adds weight and makes it difficult to get an ergonomic riding position (due to the constraints of squeezing everything into such a small space). The low rider weight means most suspension on kids' bikes does not move at all anyway. Gears should be wide ratio, with plenty of low gears. Until they are teenagers, most children won't understand how to operate a front changer effectively, so they are best avoided. Look for wide ratio cassettes instead, or hub gears. Also look for simple cable runs as this will keep the action of the shifters smooth for longer, important for small, weak hands.

Check the brakes, and accept no lesser quality than you'd be happy riding yourself. Check that the levers are reachable by small hands (Islabikes have a very nice custom-made short reach lever). Cranks should also be proportionate to the size of the bike, and that definitely means a lot shorter than adult cranks!

Islabikes (www.islabikes.co.uk) are perhaps the front-runners for well-designed children's bikes, with a range covering the age spectrum and based around lightweight frames and appropriate components. Some of the major bike ranges such as Trek and Giant have some good kid's bikes – just pay a bit more than bargain basement prices. Or try the range of German Puky kids' bikes imported by London Recumbents. Another popular option is a BMX bike – not so suited for anything like a longer ride, but they are robust, stylish and come in all qualities from dire to exquisite.

Your child may be able to ride his or her own scooter or bike from really quite a young age – scooters from two and up, and bikes from as young as three or four. But cycling will be an activity to be enjoyed in small doses – like just about everything else at that age – and in safe surroundings: at home, in the park, or on railway paths or the like, until older and wiser.

Trailerbikes

Time to move up an age bracket, and on to the stage at which children can start to contribute to propulsion. Trailerbikes are a great way to get much of the benefits of tandeming without the considerable expense – and storage issues – of actually owning a tandem. They let the child passenger fully participate in the riding experience without (yet) having the freedom to make their own traffic decisions. Normally equipped with a set of gears, trailerbikes can even be viable vehicles for longer rides or touring if you get a good one. Typically they'll adjust to fit a wide age range, somewhere between four and ten.

The 'reference standard' among trailerbikes has always (as long as I've been cycling) been the Burley Piccolo (around £350 in the UK). With its rock-solid rack-mounted pivot it tracks extremely well. I've heard that some of the cheaper models from, for example, Adams are much improved in recent years. Another good one is the Add+Bike from Hoening in Germany, imported by Bikefix for £265.

Most budget models attach to the seatpost. Do check that the pivots are adequately engineered, as there's nothing more irritating (and possibly dangerous) for both child and rider than a trailerbike leaning wonkily off to one side because the swivel bearings are worn out.

A few variations on the trailerbike theme deserve special mention:

» The Hase Trets uses a standard Weber trailer hitch to attach a two-wheeled, recumbent-seated trailer bike. Complete with harness to keep them firmly in place, it's a fearsome £755 but is a lovely bit of kit, and children love it.

» Kinetics recumbent trailerbike: this is a more-or-less one off recumbent trailerbike. Kinetics can make more to order.

» Pashley's Add-1: a two-wheeled upright trailer bike, also available in adult sizes. Sadly, the tandem version, the U plus 2, seems to have disappeared from their current range. This was a great vehicle for carrying two children, plus luggage, behind a normal bike. The Add-1 costs from £445 in the UK: see www.pashley.co.uk or Tel 01789 292 263.

Tandems

Types of tandem

There are as many types of tandem as solo bikes, but if you're looking to do a world tour by tandem you'll probably already know what you're after, so we won't go into 'standard' touring or racing machines in much depth. For now we'll concentrate on the types most appropriate for family cycling.

In the UK, anyone with an interest in tandeming should join the Tandem

Club (see Resources, later) for a very modest fee. There are also a number of specialist tandem dealers/manufacturers: in the UK these include JD Cycles in Ilkley near Leeds (JD now own the Orbit brand), St John St Cycles (for 'Thorn' tandems), MSG Bikes in Lancing and others.

The author riding a Santos tandem from JD Cycles.

Low frame 'family tandems'

With a 'small' frame, reminiscent of folding bikes, these tandems are great in their 'one-size-fits-all' versatility. With both saddles able to be adjusted over a wide range any combination of family members can use the same machine: saddles down for two children, or up for both parents. Often equipped with smaller wheels (usually 20") these machines are generally affordable, simple, and better suited to utility riding than extended tours.

Examples include the £795 Orbit Libra from JD Cycles and the rather more pricey but very nice Family Tandem range from Bike Friday. This is capable of touring – and can also dismantle into a suitcase or two for transport. Well worth a look, and available in the UK via Avon Valley Cyclery (www.foldingbikes.co.uk) amongst others. Another touring-capable option is the Bernds folding tandem pictured below: see www.bernds.de.

Childback tandems

A 'Childback' is like a normal tandem, but with the frame falling away at the back to accommodate a smaller rider. With extended seatposts a childback tandem can fit a fairly wide age-range – but even if it is outgrown, it'll be easy to sell on at a good price. A good example is the smallest-size 13"/20"

Dawes Duet, a value choice at around £575.

Triplets and more

As far as I'm aware the only company making triplets (bikes for three riders) in the UK is St John St Cycles. Their Thorn Me'n'u2 childback triplet is a popular choice with families with more than one children to transport, and at prices from £1199 it's remarkably affordable.

In the USA Santana also make three, four and even five seater vehicles, but at fairly high prices: available in the UK via JD Cycles.

Less usual tandems

The Onderwater TandemTransporter (www.onderwaterfiets.nl, pictured left), made in the Netherlands and imported by www.dutchbike. co.uk, is a tandem which puts the stoker (the non-steering rider) in front and the captain (the steerer) behind. Because the captain is usually taller, both riders get a good view. But the really clever bit is that they share the steering, giving both riders a real feeling of participation. For safety of course the captain has plenty of extra leverage. This bike is often used for special needs cycling (blind stokers can get the wind in their hair for a change!), but it makes a great family tandem too.

Similar but perhaps more minimalist is the KidzTandem from Brown Cycles in the USA (right) – though they're looking for European distributors as we go to press.

The Pino from Hase Bikes in Germany has one rider (the stoker) in a recumbent seat at the front, and the captain upright behind. Conversation is easy, luggage capacity excellent, and both riders get a good view. It's also quite a compact machine, and the latest versions also separate into two parts for transport. The front rider can have their own freewheel, or even a hand-crank unit instead of pedals. Or you can simply mount a child seat there instead. A very versatile machine, the Pino also finds many applications in all-abilities cycling. From around £2300 in the UK from several Hase dealers, and secondhand ones come up occasionally too.

Tandem technology

Stoker comfort

Sitting behind the captain, the stoker generally can't see the road ahead,

and so it's hard to react to bumps, even with verbal warnings from the captain. Shocks which hit the rear wheel can seem to travel straight up the stoker's spine – so many tandems are fitted with suspension seatposts to improve stoker comfort. Some of the modern air-suspension ones, from USE for example, are good, but even better are parallelogram-

This tandem is fitted with a Thudbuster seatpost.

linkage models such as the Cane Creek Thudbuster – not cheap but very good indeed. Add a well-chosen saddle and comfort problems should be much reduced.

Brakes

Tandems are hard on brakes: they have around twice the weight to stop with still just two wheels. The best set-up is still hotly debated amongst tandemists. Many prefer the simplicity, easy maintenance and power of V-brakes, combined perhaps with an Arai drum brake to act as a 'drag' on long descents. Magura hydraulic rim brakes are a popular alternative to V-brakes. A couple of really good rim brakes may well be fine by themselves if you ride only in fairly flat places.

As to disk brakes, opinions are divided. While some have no problems, others find that on long descents disks overheat and fail in a variety of interesting ways. Very few bicycle disk brakes are rated for tandem use: most are designed for minimum weight when used on solo bikes. Avid BB7 mechanical disks are a tandem favourite, used with the largest disks available (203 mm or 8"). If you go hydraulic, use the heaviest downhilling brake available – Hope's heaviest, or the Magura Gustav M for example.

Transporting tandems

Various ingenious devices exist to help get tandems onto the top of cars, and the Tandem Club has a comprehensive guide on its website.

Folding tandems are another option. The Multicycle full-sized models, available via JD Cycles and MSG Bikes, has a folding front section. This allows it to be

transported behind a normal car on a standard bike rack, without sticking out each side. It's a very nicely built tandem for the leisure rider, too.

Resources

»   In the UK the Tandem Club can offer invaluable advice, social riding and a regular newsletter: See www.tandem-club.org.uk or direct new membership enquiries to Peter Hallowell on 01235 525161.

»   Sheldon Brown's website has, as ever, much useful advice: www.sheldonbrown.com/family/

Special needs cycling

It's with mixed feelings that I write this chapter on special needs cycling. Not because I don't think it's a good thing to do. Rather, because special needs cycling shouldn't really seen as a separate, 'other' thing: something that most cyclists don't normally encounter or consider.

Instead I see special needs bikes as simply being at one end of a continuum of cycling. Every cyclist adapts his or her bike to suit specific needs. Special needs bikes just tend to be adapted a bit more than most. Changing your stem for a more upright model to ease a stiff back is just as much special-needs cycling as is changing your propulsion from pedals to hand-cranks as circumstances dictate.

But perhaps because the mainstream of cycling is dominated by fit, young men, designs which cater for the disabled, the elderly and infirm, or just the non-athletic, are often seen as one of cycling's more obscure niches. Yet it's a large and growing sector of the market, with hundreds of manufacturers and suppliers catering for an ever-wider range of all-abilities cyclists. There are some great people out there doing great work and who deserve full support – after all, any one of us could require their services tomorrow, next month, or next decade.

Why cycle?

The benefits of cycling for the disabled are just the same as for the able-bodied. It's fun, gives independent mobility and promotes physical and mental well-being. However, for many disabled people, these benefits have particular significance. Opportunities for exercise may be limited, and there are recognised problems of weight gain, muscle wastage and poor circulation associated with prolonged wheelchair use or a sedentary lifestyle.

Cycling can noticeably extend the speed and distance of independent movement which is possible compared to a wheelchair. And compared to motorised or electric transport, both initial and ongoing costs are minimal. Cycling can also be an enjoyable activity to share with able-bodied friends or carers.

Even when full independence is not possible, the therapeutic benefits of cycling are clear. Many first-time riders explain the feeling as exhilarating, empowering, challenging. Centres across the world are now regularly introducing new people to the joys and benefits of cycling – as well as putting many cyclists who are no longer able to ride a standard bike back on the road.

Finding information and advice

There are plenty of places willing and able to give advice and information. There's no substitute for getting expert advice and trying out a range of machines for yourself. So rather than agonise for ages over this guide or spending hours on the internet, do contact the dealers and organisations which are there to help – and get yourself a test-ride!

» Charities/organisations: See our listing later on for details of who does what. In the UK at least, all-ability cycling projects tend to be regionally-based, so some travel may well be required. However, it could well be worth the effort: many of these projects now have well-equipped fleets of specialised cycles, and experienced staff (often volunteers) who can advise on their use and possible modification. Most often you'll be able to try out a range of bikes in safe surroundings to find what suits your particular needs.

» Dealers and manufacturers: again, these are listed later. There are now a good number of dealers and manufacturers in the special needs cycling field, and they'll naturally be happy to advise on how their products can help get you moving. Many will be equipped to make custom modifications to suit their customers.

» Don't necessarily take the first advice you're given: not every dealer will have a full range. If you're after something very particular you may have to hunt around. Often I hear of people having machines expensively custom-built when a commercial model already exists. It's shame to reinvent the wheel when an existing machine is presumably cheaper and designed with the benefit of valuable development and testing experience.

» Dealers and charity organisations will be able to advise on possible sources of funding to help get you the bike you need: this varies so widely from country to country and from year to year I'm not going to even try giving details here. Ask an expert!

» Events: Cycling events such as the York Cycle Show and others often have special-needs displays, at which dealers, manufacturers and often charitable organisations are on hand to advise. A good way to get a quick test-ride! Similar displays may also be on offer at non-cycling-specific disability events.

» Racing handcycles can be seen (in the UK) at many running races and BHPC HPV race events — see the UK Handcycling Association info later. In other countries there are similar organisations, with the USA in particular having an active handcycle racing scene.

» Internet: There is a huge amount of information on the web about all aspects of special needs cycling – most manufacturers and dealers have websites, as do most of the organisations active in the field. We'll list a number in this article, but there are very many more.

Mailing lists such as http://groups.yahoo.com/group/handcyclists/ where users and potential users can exchange information can also be very useful.

Types of bike

Many special needs cyclists use the same bikes as anyone else, slightly adapted, or just for different reasons. Many of the specialised designs we've featured in other chapters can be very useful – and riding a machine not necessarily seen as 'for the disabled' can be an attractive idea.

For some cases, machines designed specifically for the purpose are required; these machines can often be used by the able-bodied.

We won't cover 'therapy bikes' in great detail – these are machines intended for the very severely disabled and particularly for children. Usually owned and operated by institutions or charities, there are all sorts of solutions available – we can only scratch the surface here.

More-or-less standard cycles useful for special needs cycling

Tandems

Tandems are ideal when one rider, for whatever reason, can't control a bike sufficiently well to be safe – but can still pedal fine. So for many years now tandems have offered a great way for the visually impaired to cycle – and race, and go on extended tours.

Tandems are also ideal for those with learning difficulties, balance and co-ordination problems to enjoy cycling in safety. Small-frame tandems can be ideal to get children out and about, while remaining fully under the control of the 'captain'. There's more on tandems in the 'Family Cycling' Chapter.

Designs which place the non-steering rider at the front have additional benefits for supervision and safety – and also make conversation between the riders easier. These designs are usually intended for child front riders. Suppliers include Kidztandem, Onderwater, and Van Raam.

Low step-through bikes

For some riders with limited mobility but good balance a standard bike may be perfectly OK – but getting on and off may be a problem. There are designs around now which have a very low 'step-through' indeed, easing the access problem significantly. There's even one machine from Germany where the frame wraps around the side, so you don't have to step over anything at all to get onto the saddle.

The Epple Millennium from Germany: see www.epple-bikes.de for more details.

Semi-recumbents

Semi-recumbent bikes have a seat rather than a saddle, but

you sit very upright rather than leaned back. This can be ideal for those who find a conventional bike uncomfortable. The lower riding position means that feet can be put flat and stable on the ground when you stop, and an upright riding position keeps the neck straight and puts no weight on the wrists. It can take a few minutes to get used to the 'light' steering on most such machines, and they do suit a more leisurely pace. They're also known as 'Crank Forward' bikes. RANS in America make a wide range (see www.feetforwardbikes.co.uk).

The RANS feet-forward design gives an upright riding position, with no neck strain and no weight on the wrists.

Upright trikes, tandem trikes and conversion kits

One of the most popular machines at most special needs cycling centres is the simple upright tricycle. It has the familiar looks of a 'normal bike' but the three wheels provide stability. Trikes are available in all types, from shoppers to racing-quality machines – and some have low step-through, too. As for able-bodied riders, trikes can be very practical machines, with load-carrying capacity between the rear wheels.

Affordable upright trikes are supplied by, for example, Mission Cycles (www.missioncycles.co.uk).

Tandem trikes are also available (at a price): these can combine the benefits of tandem riding with the lack of balance worries of a trike layout. Manufacturers include Longstaff Cycles (www.longstaffcycles.com).

A cheaper option than a purpose-built trike may be a conversion kit, offered by several manufacturers, including Altena-Bike who make the 'Opus3' kit pictured: www.altena-bike.nl.

It's worth bearing in mind that the stability of upright trikes can be a bit limited in fast cornering unless the riders are expert and agile.

Some models put the two wheels at the front for greater stability (and, most would agree, easier handling). These do tend to be rather more expensive, though. London Recumbents (www.londonrecumbents.co.uk) import good ones, the T-bike range.

Recumbent trikes and tandem trikes

Increasingly popular with able-bodied cyclists, recumbent trikes are usually very stable, and in contrast to upright trikes have a full seat, rather than a saddle, to support the rider. They can be ideal for riders with back problems. They do tend to be a bit more costly than upright trikes.

Tandem recumbent trikes can be particularly useful for special needs cycling: the rear seat is a very stable platform, and can often be adapted to offer either hand-crank or pedal drive. The commercial models are mainly intended for able-bodied touring, and so are relatively light with good performance.

Side-by-side machines such as the ZEM or 2Can or the Doublerider (as pictured) offer additional benefits of easy conversation and sociability, but the width of these machines can put some riders off for use on the roads.

Up/down tandems

There are really only two available bikes which fit in this category, but they're worthy of particular note. The first is the Hase Spezialraeder Pino: this combines an upright rear rider (who steers) with a recumbent front seat and either pedals or hand-cranks. Both riders get a good view to the front and can converse easily as their heads are close together. The rear rider does the balancing, and the front rider can freewheel at will. This can be a high-performance bike suitable for touring. It's made in Germany, but there are plenty of UK importers.

The second is the Strada, again from Germany. It's a similar layout, but

with a wide-track 'tricycle' front end for stability. This would be ideal where the able-bodied upright rider can't fully control a two-wheeler – perhaps because of the weight of a front rider with balance or control problems. I don't know of an importer at present.

Loadbikes

Many of the machines covered in the chapter on load-carrying can be useful for special-needs cyclists. Some can simply carry a person in a wheelchair as 'cargo' – others are particularly suited to carrying disabled children in safety and comfort. In general, machines with the load-bed in front of the rider are particularly suitable, so that the disabled passenger is in the rider's view, and conversation is easy.

Rickshaw-type machines can of course carry passengers of any ability.

'Standard' child trailers are often suitable for transporting young children with disabilities, perhaps with seat and seatbelt modifications to keep the occupant secure.

Trailerbikes and trailer trikes

Single-wheeled trailerbikes are only really designed for children, as the weight of an adult could be too much for the towing bike to handle. We covered these in the Family Cycling chapter.

Trailer trikes are also available for adults. Try Mission Cycles: the Piggyback 24 pictured costs around £280.

Electric assist

Electric-assist systems can be fitted to most cycles these days – so providing extra power on demand. This can be particularly useful for those whose strength can swiftly be exhausted – it's a 'get you home' measure. A bit of electric assistance can also be great when one rider is doing most of the work on, say, an adapted tandem – particularly in the hills.

Most manufacturers will have their own systems, but for retrofitting to an existing bike the German Heinzmann kits, imported into the UK by Emotive Control Systems, are generally thought to be a reliable choice: see http://www.emotivecontrolsystems.co.uk.

Special-needs specific cycles

Wheelchair tandems

Along with handcycles, these are probably the most familiar 'special needs' cycles around. Combining a wheelchair front end with a detachable bicycle rear end, they're a way to share a bike ride with anyone who can't ride themselves. The layouts put your heads close together for easy conversation, and both share the view to the front.

Usually the wheelchair is quick-releasable from the bicycle rear end, so when you reach your destination the passenger can move around independently.

Now available from a multitude of suppliers, the original and best-known of this type is the Hoening Duet. A host of adaptations, supports and the like are available. The rear bicycle part is often equipped with an electric-assist system, especially in hilly areas, as the single rider must propel the weight of two people and a fairly heavy bike.

A variation on this theme is the 'Discoverer', which has the wheelchair in a 'sidecar' configuration beside the bike rider.

Handcycles

Alongside the wheelchair tandem the other iconic 'special-needs' bike

Varna racing handcycle in action

is the handcycle. Powering the wheels by arm-power rather than pedals, these machines offer greater efficiency and speed than the usual 'wheeling' of a chair ever can. A wide variety of types is available:

» Racing handcycles are built for speed and performance, and with a fit rider can be quite capable of keeping up with able-bodied (non-racing) cyclists on a ride. Usually low-slung and lightweight. Visit a handcycle race, or check out some of the handcycling websites we list below for details of the various brands on offer. Many are made in USA and Canada, where the racing scene is well-established, but there are plenty of importers.

» Add-on handcycle units attach in front of a more-or-less conventional wheelchair, usually in quick-release fashion, and provide a relatively cheap and simple way to add efficiency and mobility. There are a multitude of models available (mostly, wheelchair and drive unit are bought together) and all levels of gearing etc are available. These units can also be combined with electric-assist systems.

» Side by side handcycle trikes or quads are often used by cycling centres: they offer great sociability in a very stable platform. However, the only ones I've seen have been very heavy 'institutional' types – good for having a go, but not much use as transport.

The One-Off All-Terrain Handcycle

» Offroad handcycles are a bit of a rare breed: I know of a number of prototypes and proposals, but just one commercial one: the US-made One-Off Titanium All-Terrain Handcycle. A quite remarkable machine – see www.titaniumarts.com for more details. There's an annual World Championship for riders.

An even more amazing vehicle is the 'Snow-Pod', a tracked, hand-cranked machine used to ascend large snow-covered mountains: see the makers' website at www.mobilityeng.com for details. They also make an interesting two-wheeled handcycle – almost all others have three wheels.

The images and stories on those last two websites are a great demonstration that you need accept no limits just because you're hand-cranking not pedalling.

Special needs adaptations

Often a rider's existing bike can be adapted to take account of a special need, rather than replacing it with a custom machine. Here's a few of the available items:

» Pedal plates are used to keep the rider's foot firmly in position. This can be important for safety.

» Adjustable cranks are useful where the range of motion on one or more limbs is restricted – so the pedal or hand-crank needs to move through a smaller arc.

» Freewheeling cranks are useful to keep a non-functioning foot in place, while the bike is driven by the other, fully-functioning limb.

» Pedal spacers are used when extra clearance is required for feet.

» Fixed wheel: it can sometimes be a good idea to have no freewheel in the system, so the pedals turn whenever the bike is moving. Especially when one limb is weaker than the other, it keeps the pedals turning evenly, the inertia of the bike carrying it smoothly past the 'dead spots' at top and bottom of the pedal stroke. A fixed gear can also be a very convenient 'reverse' – getting a trike to move backwards can otherwise be tricky without dismounting.

» One-handed operation: it's relatively simple to move all controls to one hand. The brake lever can be modified (both for cable and hydraulics) to actuate two brakes at once, and gearing controls are usually straightforward. A Schlumpf bottom-bracket gear unit can be helpful to reduce the 'clutter', as it's shifted with the heel and requires no hand controls.

» Hip, back and neck supports: these can be useful where a rider may need some extra support while riding to avoid possible injury – or just to increase comfort.

Organisations

Numerous charities are involved in the special needs cycling field, many with full-time experts and fleets of bikes. They should be your first port of call for advice. We'll list specialist dealers and manufacturers next.

» Wheels for All: Well-established group offering cycling for all at 21 centres across the country: ring their 'hotline' on 01925 234213 or see www.cycling. org.uk for full details. They also have some interesting and useful publications on offer.

» London Cycling Campaign produce an All-Abilities Cycling Guide, a 16 page, A5 guide to machines and resources in the UK. It's available free from the LCC, or downloadable from their website. Tel 020 7928 7220 or see www.lcc. org.uk. They also have a more up-to-date fact sheet.

» Bikeability: Ipswich-based special-needs group with a large fleet of bikes and team of volunteers. Bikeability: www.bikeability.org.uk

» CycleMagic: Leicester-based cycle promotion charity which includes special-needs activities: good fleet of bikes and huge workshop in safe surroundings for try-out. Rides, advice and sales. Tel 0116 262 5551 or see www.cyclemagic.org.uk

» Companion Cycling is a not-for-profit scheme based in Bushy Park in South-West London and has a fleet of mostly side-by-side tandems, which allow all to go for traffic-free rides in company. Tel 07961 344545 or see www.companioncycling.org.uk

» Company of Cyclists produce a free info sheet listing special needs cycling resources: they also sometimes do special-needs roadshows. Tel 01904 778 080 or see www.companyofcyclists.com

» Tandem Club: The UK Tandem Club has a Disabilities Liaison Officer who may be able to help with queries related to disabled people and to visually handicapped cyclists. Contact Alan Tibble: Tel 01522 695781.

» Gateway Wheelers: Disability cycling group in the Chester-le-Street/Tees Valley area: have a good range of machines and offer rides, advice and more. See www.gatewaywheelers.org.uk or phone 0791 390 5422

» Handcycling Association UK: promote handcycling, both recreational and competitive. Their website lists events, has advice on buying, and more. See www.handcycling.org.uk

» Crank it up! Bradford-based group with a range of cycles. See www.crank-it-up.org.uk or phone 07835 840989.

Manufacturers/Suppliers

Attempting to offer even a reasonably comprehensive list is a mammoth task, especially with the limited space available here. The ones listed here should be a good start.

A Speedy Tandem imported by Bromakin Wheelchairs. A lever mechanism allows the wheelchair user to attach and detach unaided from the cycle front end. For heavier riders hydraulic brakes can be fitted the wheelchair wheels, linked to the front bike. Versatile fittings mean that usually it's possible to use an existing wheelchair.

In the UK:

» Bikecare: offer tricycle conversion kits and a range of family cycling and special needs cycles. 92 The Avenue, March, Cambridgeshire. PE15 9PR. Tel 01354 660049 Website www.bikecare.co.uk

» Bromakin Wheelchairs: major, established supplier of wheelchairs and handcycles, with a huge range. Includes imported machines from Varna (Canada), Speedy (Germany) and more. Everything from basic bolt-on hand-cranks to top-class racers. Bromakin Wheelchairs, 12 Prince William Road, Loughborough, Leicestershire LE11 0GU UK. Tel 01509 217569 or Fax 01509 233954 or see www.bromakin.co.uk

» Chevron: UK manufacturer of handcycles and an adult upright trike: Brunswick Business Park, 18 Summers Road, Liverpool L3 4BL. Tel: 0151 707 1146 Fax: 0151 707 0353 www.chevronwheelchairs.co.uk

» Cyclemakers (also known as Logic Engineering Concepts): make the Victorian and Discoverer tandems, and the Co-Star tandem, and also offer a custom engineering service. See www.cyclemakers.co.uk or Tel 01562 731 355

» Cyclone Mobility and Fitness: Sell the Tracker range of handcycles along with a wide range of wheelchairs and other vehicles: Cyclone, Freepost, Unit 5, Apex Court, Bassendale Road, Croft Business Park, Bromborough CH62 3RE. Tel :0151 346 2310 Fax : 0151 346 2311

» EPC Wheelchairs: large UK retailer importing machines from Invacare and impressive racing machines from Sopur, and also making a few themselves. Lots of electric-assist etc options too. EPC Head Office: 43 Alexandra Road, Farnborough, Hampshire, GU14 6BS. Tel: 01252 547939 Fax: 01252 377588. Website is www.epc-wheelchairs.co.uk

» London Recumbents: offer try-out and advice in Dulwich Park in London. Distributors for Hase, Hoening and others. Their website is particularly good if you're looking for possible sources of funding. Tel 0208 299 6636 or see www.londonrecumbents.co.uk

» Longstaff Cycles: As well as making lovely custom tandems and tandem trikes, Longstaffs produce affordable trikes and tandems for children and adults under the 'Cyclon' brand. Trike conversion kits are also available, as are many crank adapters and other fitments, and machines can be constructed to suit individual requirements. Longstaff Cycles, Albert St, Chesterton, Newcastle-under-Lyme, Staffs ST5 7JF. Tel 01782 561 966 www.longstaffcycles.co.uk

» Pashley Cycles: Manufacturers of many useful family and special needs cycles. Contact them on 01789 292 263 or see www.pashley.co.uk for more details.

» WiseWheels: Malcolm and Mary Jones supply specialist cycles to children and adults with disabilities or mobility problems. UK distributors for specialised equipment from Draisin, Triaid, Hoening and Berg Toys. Tel/ Fax 01295 770806 or see www.wisewheels.co.uk

» Quest 88: UK distributors for Draisin bikes and trikes, Petra Running Bikes and Berg Go-Karts. See www.childrenstricycles.com or www. quest88.com or phone 01952 463050

Draisin trike, imported by Quest88

Workbikes

Why carry loads?

There are many reasons for carrying loads by bike. Cycle couriers do it for a living. You may want to carry a serious load of shopping, carry a family's luggage on a cycle tour, or transport a pet to the vet... the list goes on.

It's possible to carry some fairly incredible loads by bicycle, but you do need the right equipment:

» For very large loads, or for daily, intensive use, it's usually worth spending out on a specially-designed load-carrying cycle.

» For more occasional large loads, a trailer may be more appropriate.

» And don't forget that with some good panniers, you can carry a surprising amount on your standard bicycle, without the expense and storage problems which come from an additional bike or trailer.

Children are a special case, and we've already covered this in an earlier chapter. Many of the machines presented here will be suitable for child-carrying, of course, perhaps with minor modifications to fit childseats or the like.

Safety is vital when carrying unusual loads: be absolutely sure that your load is secure, your brakes are up to the job and that whatever you're using to carry the weight is strong enough for the task. Before you take your loaded-up machine out into traffic, I strongly suggest trying a few emergency stops, riding over a bump or two and giving the load a good shake. Keep the speed down. Most machines and trailers come with a recommended weight limit: stick to it. Mark the extremities of overhanging loads with a flag and, if at night, with lights. With common sense, load-carrying by bike is safe and fun.

That said, let's take a look at some of the load-carrying cycles and trailers you can buy.

Special-purpose bikes and trikes

Ideal for extra-heavy or extra-bulky loads, or for day-in, day-out load-carrying, these bikes are designed with load-carrying in mind. They aren't usually cheap, but you are paying for industrial strength and durability, and the peace of mind of using a professional, tested design.

Cycles Maximus 'One Less Car'

Designed as both a modern rickshaw and a heavy load-carrier, the Cycles Maximus 'One Less Car' trike is deservedly regarded as perhaps the best heavy-duty worktrike around. I've ridden the ones belonging to York's couriers and recycling teams and can say first-hand that they really are excellent.

Braking is tremendous with two hydraulic Hope disks at the back and Magura rim brakes on the front. Wheels are massively strong, with moped rear wheels and a 48-spoke BMX front. The 42-speed transmission uses a final step-down drive to the differential (both rear wheels are driven). There are plenty of really, really low gears, yet

it can also move pretty fast with traffic when necessary.

The steel chassis has attachment points for a variety of load or people-carrying modules, which can be fitted or exchanged in minutes. The flat-bed can be fitted with an effective fabric canopy for weather protection and/or advertising space.

The only downside is that with smaller loads the capacity of the Max is rather wasted. It's a relatively slow and bulky machine to pedal round if you're just carrying small items. Unladen weight is around 45 kg, plus around 25 kg for the load-carrying back.

The trike is rated to carry 250 kg, including the rider. In my experience this is realistic, and this vehicle is one of the few ways to carry that sort of weight in real safety.

It's available direct from Cycles Maximus: Tel 01225 319414 or see www. cyclesmaximus.com. Prices start around £2400 for a flatbed trike, more for other body options.

Burrows Engineering 8-Freight

With a load area of around 45x80cm, the 8-Freight can take four standard A4-sized boxes comfortably, with two more strapped on top if need be. It's also good for awkward or bulky loads, with a flat load bed over the 20" rear wheel.

The 8-Freight is a very light, fast bike for the loads it carries. As a two-wheeler, it can get through gaps much more easily than a trike, and it's light

enough to be easily manhandled if need be. Mike Burrows will customise the load area, and can even build fibre-glass boxes or carriers if required.

The drum brakes with one-sided wheel supports are Burrows trademarks, and should give reliable weatherproof braking, especially now he's switched to the larger 90 mm drums for the front. For the money, it's a lot of load-bike, and is a versatile and fast way to carry all but the largest of loads. Available via Bikefix or direct from Mike Burrows, for around £1250. Burrows Engineering has no internet presence, so call him on 01603 721700.

Longtail bikes

Bikes with an extended rear rack area have come to be known as 'Longtails'. It's an increasingly popular format, perhaps because it looks pretty much 'normal': like a standard bike but longer. Unlike the 8-Freight, these bikes use a full-sized rear wheel. This means that large loads have to be either placed on one or the other side off-balance, or balanced rather high up over the rear rack – not ideal. But it's good for smaller loads, and also the format lends itself well to

carrying a passenger on the back. There are currently four models available, but prototypes and rumours from trade shows suggest more may be coming soon.

Xtracycle

Originally designed as a load-carrying modification for bikes in developing countries, the Xtracycle's 'Free Radical' is a relatively cheap and easy way to

add serious capacity to any MTB. The bolt-on subframe extends the bike to a bit less than tandem length, and provides a comfortable bench for a passenger to sit on. The standard version comes with some fabric bag-type containers each side, into which you're presumably meant to dump

shopping bags and the like. Maybe in California, where it was made, but in the UK most cyclists would prefer just to be able to attach a whole load of panniers instead – which you can't without making your own fixings for it.

Other attachments are available to carry surfboards or other long loads. The Free Radical adds around 4.3 kg to the weight of your bike, complete with standard accessories. It is rated to 90 kg, although even on a solid MTB frame, the machine starts feeling a bit flexible when heavily loaded.

Price: from £360 in the UK, from Loads Better: Tel 0845 8682459 or see www.thisisloadsbetter.co.uk. The Xtracycle manufacturers are at: www.xtracycle.com

Yuba Mundo

The Yuba is a heavy-duty longtail, designed again for use in both developing

and developed countries. With a massive 15 mm solid rear axle and extra-heavy spokes, and a super robust frame, it's a real workhorse, weighing around 28 kg. The price is good (from £475) but specification is basic (though easily upgraded). Rated capacity is a massive 200 kg on the wide rear rack, so it can even carry passengers if necessary.

The 2008 model's rear rack was too wide to easily fit child seats, but it'll be narrower for 2009, and the rack rails will also let you hook panniers straight on.

Distributed in the UK by Loads Better: Tel 0845 8682459 or see www. thisisloadsbetter.co.uk. The manufacturers are at: www.yubaride.com

Kona Ute

A longtail from mountain bike makers Kona, who have dealers all over, making this one of the easiest long-tails to get hold of. It's much lighter-duty than the Yuba, but probably tough enough for non-extreme use and the bike itself is certainly lighter, too. It has disk brakes and 700c wheels (a strange choice, weaker than 26"). Rack rails are too fat for pannier hooks, sadly. Retails in the UK at around £580. Weight is 16.8 kg, but strangely, they don't seem to publish a load capacity. See www.konabikes.co.uk for more details.

Surly Big Dummy

Available as frame and forks only, this longtail bike from US makers Surly is designed to take Xtracycle rear end parts, so that any accessories which fit the Xtracycle will fit the Surly. But the all-in-one frame design is more rigid. At £750 for frame and forks it's an expensive option – and you or your local bike shop will still need to buy all the bits to build it into a bike. The 'army' version pictured was a trade show special, incidentally.

Via any Surly dealer: see www.surlybikes.com for a list.

Front loading trikes

A popular formula in mainland Europe is the trike with two wheels at the front and a large load box in between. This layout is well suited to city traffic, with the widest part in easy view, and with great street presence. They do however tend to be heavy, difficult to manhandle and hard work on hills. Often gearing and braking may require upgrades, especially in hilly terrain.

Christiania trikes

A Danish creation, the Christiania has been made and refined for decades now. It's a simple design, with the two front wheels fixed to the box. To steer, the bike bends in the middle, with the pivot designed to slightly lean the rider into the curves. There are twin drum or disk brakes, controlled via a 'lever' running all the way along the handlebar, and a back-pedal brake. Usually hub gears are fitted. On some versions the front part detaches quickly and can be used as a hand-cart or stroller. There are several boxes available, from a standard low open box to a full-enclosed post box. There's also a design especially for carrying children.

A capable and very reliable medium-capacity load-carrier, my only reservation about the Christiania is its handling at speed. The pivot-in-the-

middle steering can tend to wobble, and any problems are exacerbated if the brakes are less than perfectly balanced. Nonetheless, for normal loadbike or child-carrying use, it's fine.

From £930.

Available via Velorution in London: Tel 020 7723 2409 or see www. velorution.biz. Manufacturer: www.christianiabikes.dk

Dutchbike.co.uk Cargotrike

Rather along the same lines is the Cargotrike from Netherlands workbike specialists bakfiets.nl. It seems to get good reviews as a solid performer. From £1455 direct from www.dutchbike.co.uk or phone 0777 273 8899.

Nihola

While both Christiania and Bakfiets trikes steer the entire front end, the Nihola from Denmark steers just the wheels. This makes it much less ponderous, especially when loaded, and it also does better at speed. It is a bit more expensive, so do try a test ride to see whether the performance is worth it. I'd say it is.

Available, like the others, in various sizes and configurations. In the UK, it's from £1800 via London Recumbents. The manufacturer is www.nihola. dk

Front Cargo Bikes

Bikes with a cargo area in front share many of the advantages we've just explained for trikes – but they're lighter, cheaper, and are easier to get through gaps in traffic, doorways and the like. Most will come with a sturdy stand so that they stay stable as you load them up.

Dutchbike.co.uk Bakfiets

Perhaps the original modern interpretation of the idea is the Dutch Bakfiets, a favourite for both child and load carrying. It's solidly made, has predictable handling and plenty of accessories such as rain canopies are available. In the UK, it costs from £1280 via www. dutchbike.co.uk or phone 0777 273 8899.

An upgraded version of this machine is available via Henry Workcycles in Amsterdam, a workbike specialist dealer run by an ex-pat American. Well worth a visit if you can channel-hop over. Their Bakfiets has upgraded brakes, lighting and a nicer rear wheel. See www.workcycles.com for details.

Manufacturer's website is at www.bakfiets.nl.

Larry vs Harry Bullitt

More aimed at pure load-carrying, and also aiming at a younger, more stylish set than some of the traditional load carriers is the Bullitt from

Copenhagen company Larry vs Harry. The aluminium frame makes it light

(around 23 kg) and rigid, and the riding position is much more leaned-over and sporty than most. From 1700 Euros, sadly no distributor in the UK as yet. See www.larryvsharry.com

Long John

If you like the traditional look then the classic Long John is hard to beat. It's built to last and has a 100 kg load capacity. The price in the UK is around £1600 inc. VAT, from Loads Better: Tel 0845 8682459 or see www.thisisloadsbetter.co.uk

Trailers

Many of the trailers people use for load-carrying were originally child-carriers – see the Family chapter. But there are also quite a number of specially-designed cargo trailers for loads of all shapes and sizes…

Bikes at Work

The trailers from Bikes At Work in the USA are simply the last word in large trailers. They may not have a UK importer at the moment, but they just can't be left out.

After a recent redesign, their load trailer is better than ever. It's a modular system, which assembles from a series of aluminium extrusions to form a trailer essentially as large as you want – the 64" (1.6 m) long model is a very good size and their most popular. Rated at 135 kg load capacity (though I'd

say that's rather more than you'd really want to do an emergency stop with, especially in hilly terrain).

Among the things I particularly rate about this trailer, beyond its huge versatility, is the solidity of the drawbar and hitch. An insufficiently stiff drawbar can flex and oscillate as you ride along, 'pulsing' the load disconcertingly. No chance of that here. And the hitch is extremely low (below chainstay height) and also solidly made.

Available direct from the manufacturer in the USA. The trailers themselves are very reasonably priced – from the dollar equivalent of around £200 currently. And shipping to the UK won't be too painful, as the disassembled trailer flatpacks well. Tel 001 515 233 6120 or see www. bikesatwork.com

Carryfreedom Y-Frame and City

Carryfreedom from Scotland are good people to talk to if you want a custom trailer made – they are happy to create one-off solutions. They also make two 'standard' trailers. The first is the Y-Frame, a basic load platform with light aluminium frame and plywood load bed. The frame can be extended by inserting extra sections, and a wider rear axle is also available, so the trailer does expand for larger loads. Various boxes are available, too. 45 kg limit, price around £180.

Their second trailer is the ingenious folding City model. This works as a handcart or trailer – and if you remove the bag (which converts to a

backpack) both wheels and drawbar fold away within the trailer. Ideal as a companion to a folding bike, and will get on public transport where many others won't. From around £250. Both available via dealers or direct from Carryfreedom: Tel 0845 456 0928 or see www.carryfreedom.com

Roland trailers

Roland from Germany make a wide range, from basic plastic boxes
on wheels at not much over
£100 to this, their largest 'Maxi'
model. It's a very light modular
design, so you can build up the
sidewalls as high as you like.
Top quality kit, but not cheap at
£300+. From Bikes and Trailers,
www.bikesandtrailers.co.uk

Extrawheel

A very clever trailer from
Poland, extremely light and with
a highly ingenious hitch system.
It uses a standard front wheel to
match the one in your bike – so
you have an instant emergency
spare. The version shown uses
mesh bags to hold your luggage –

for 2009 there's a version onto which you can mount panniers direct. From
around £150 via several dealers. Distributors are www.cyclesense.co.uk,
manufacturer is at www.extrawheel.eu

BOB Trailers

A trailer that's inspired many
others, the BOB YAK's single-
wheel design and clever hitch
system, which replaces the towing
bike's rear quick-release skewer,

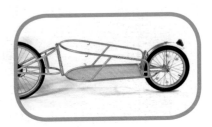

have made it a perennial favourite. It's about the only trailer you can realistically take off-road, but it's also lightweight and robust enough to tour with. Limited to around 35 kg capacity, that's nonetheless plenty for most purposes. Hard to fault, and deservedly popular. A suspended version is available for off-roaders, too. Available from many dealers, for around £250. US manufacturer's website is www.bobtrailers.com

Revolution/Mission

A Far Eastern version of the one-wheeled trailer, this same trailer is available via a number of suppliers who re-badge it, including Mission Cycles (www.missioncycles. co.uk) and Edinburgh Bikes (www. edinburghbicycle.com). It's quite a bit cheaper, at around £125, and also folds down flat for storage or transport, which can be handy. Fit and finish may not quite match the BOB, but given the price I wouldn't quibble.

Mule trailer

This £99 two-wheel load trailer is also sold under a number of names, but most usually the 'Mule'. Users seem generally happy, although some criticise the hitch design. A good bargain choice. More suppliers than you can

shake a stick at – just search online for 'Mule trailer'.

Bike Hod

If you need to use your trailer as a handcart, then a high hitch makes a perfect handle. The Bike Hod is an ideal shopping trolley-cum-trailer – you

won't want to load it above 35 kg or so but for lighter loads it's a well-behaved trailer that can carry some surprisingly bulky loads. Do be careful over bumps; it does tip over rather easily, especially unladen. But it is very convenient indeed to have a trailer smart enough to take into shops with you, just like a shopping trolley. Prices start at around £200, from Bikes and Trailers: Tel 01273 480 479 Website www.bikesandtrailers.co.uk

Radical Design Cyclone

The Radical Cyclone is a contender for 'best touring trailer'. It's a trailer in the form of a large 100 litre framed bag, with quick-release drawbar and wheels – and once these are removed, it's enough like a bag to escape the usual anti-trailer discrimination on public transport. It's also light (5.5 kg) and can carry up to 40 kg. The hitch is clever and neat, too, and should fit almost any bike. A top quality trailer, and the UK price at around £320 reflects this. From Futurecycles or Bikefix in the UK, or see the manufacturer's website at www.radicaldesign.nl

Touring

Touring is one of cycling's greatest pleasures, and even if you can only manage it once in a while it's an experience you'll never forget. This chapter is not so much a buyer's guide as a collection of ideas and tips which I hope will be useful for anyone planning on travelling by bike.

Why cycle tour?

I think most (mostly male) cyclists – and I'm no exception – must at some time in their lives have attempted to persuade a partner of the joys and excitement of touring cycling. It's not always an easy 'sell': It'll be hard work! I'll get cold and wet and miserable! You'll get me in a tent over my dead body!

Luckily, the reality of cycle touring is that it can be as easy and luxurious – or as tough and challenging – as you care to make it. Certainly even the least rugged of riders could find little to object to in a gentle, flat tour, with easy daily stages between good hotels and restaurants, all luggage carried and a solicitous tour guide on hand to solve any problem. On the other hand, there are people who ride across deserts, cut toothbrushes in half to save weight and advocate carrying just three socks (two to wear, one in the wash).

For most the balance is somewhere in between, and will be decided by a complex mix of budget, destination and personal tastes. And, whether you're travelling solo, as a couple, a group, or a family…

Accommodation

The choice here isn't just about money. It'll be affected by the types of accommodation available where you're going, and on how much 'stuff' you want to carry with you.

Camping is the heavyweight option: carrying tent, sleeping bag and optionally cooking gear won't just slow you down on hills, it'll make the whole bike more cumbersome. On the other hand, especially in wilderness areas where you can 'wild camp', it gives you unequalled versatility. It does require a certain amount of organisation to get yourself set up, luggage packed away and food cooking, all at the end of a ride, but it's amazing how quickly a routine can be established. And, of course, having camping gear with you doesn't stop you staying at other forms of accommodation whenever you fancy.

If you're staying indoors, your luggage is limited to clothing, journey food, a toolkit and maps: much less of a load.

But let me put in an extra plea for readers to really, seriously consider camping. When you've been cycling through glorious countryside, with the wind in your hair and eyes on the horizon, it's one big let-down if at the end of the day you wind up in an anonymous guest room, with the news on the TV and walls around you. Somehow staying in a tent keeps the magic going, doesn't dump you back into urban reality in the same way. It's a bigger adventure, and even if you do lack a few home comforts, after a few nights you'll wish it would never end.

Organised tours

I must admit here that I've never been on a proper organised cycling holiday. I've never even been particularly tempted. Friends who have done it have enjoyed it though, and one of the main attractions for many is the sociability. Also, there is often no route-finding to worry about, and luggage can be carried for you, too.

Self-arranged

Travelling solo or as a couple, for a week or more, my strategy is this:

» Choose a destination that won't be completely booked up with tourists, and sort out transport to and fro for the times available.

» Check out any other transport, such as trains, that you might need to return to your airport or ferry port or whatever.

» Get to your destination area, and stay somewhere in a town the first night. Buy lots of good local maps, ask advice, pick up useful tourist info.

» Plan a vague route, and set off. Do detail route planning 'on the fly' day by day, guessing which are the scenic routes from contours and markings on large-scale maps. As time goes on you'll meet people who can give more detailed route advice.

» End each day in a town or, if camping, at a campsite (get a list!). As long as it's a town of any reasonable size, and outside peak season, I don't usually bother booking ahead.

» In the evening, plan the next day's route. If there's no obvious midday stop it would be as well to get some food next morning for lunch.

This rather haphazard approach may not work for everyone: I know some cycle tourists who are happier meticulously planning every turn, booking every stay in advance and thoroughly researching the menus of food-stops along the way. I prefer to be open to opportunities and flexible.

Choosing a folding or portable bike as your steed certainly makes it easier to trust to luck, as there's always a backup plan. If there turns out to be no accommodation in the place you've stopped, you can always just fold the bikes up and take a bus, train or taxi to get a lift somewhere else.

Maps and books and online info

A large-scale map is a beautiful thing, and a source of fascination for the touring cyclist. I have no hesitation at all in spending money on large-scale maps – I think of them as cyclists' petrol money. If you do want to save, an old standby is to get a motoring atlas from a remainders bookshop for a few pounds, and just tear out the pages you need and carry them with you. That will show you most of the roads, but you'll miss out on so much.

The UK's Landranger series, at 1:50,000, are pretty much ideal for cycling, and most countries will have equivalents. At this scale you can see useful features like post offices, youth hostels, pubs, phone boxes and the like, and there'll be sufficient information to get a very good idea of where the quiet roads are. Combine one of these with a gazetteer-style guide to local attractions and you're set to go.

On a longer tour you'll end up with quite a collection: in two weeks in Ireland recently I ended up with ten maps. Any longer and it would have been worth posting them home – this is a good idea for any spare kit or souvenirs you accumulate along the way.

The weight of a map collection is perhaps the most convincing argument for that much-maligned technology, satellite navigation. Using GPS satellites, handle-bar mounted navigation devices can be pre-programmed with your route, offering directions at junctions and scrolling maps for browsing. Models change very quickly, but Garmin seems to be a long-running favourite brand for many. If you're a high-mileage, high-tech sort of cyclist this can work very well, but it's a matter of taste. I'll stick to my maps for now...

Finally – I know the internet isn't for everyone, but it is an amazing repository of cycle tour reports. With no constraint on space or need to convince a publisher, anyone can tell the world about their holiday. This means that for almost any destination you'll find someone who has cycled there already, often with useful experiences or information to share. The current favourite site for online trip reports seems to be www.crazyguyonabike. com. Also a good place to look for equipment reviews.

For inspiration rather than reference it's hard to beat a good travel book. Just go to your local library or bookshop to find a host of cycle travel writing. I well remember reading the amazing stories of Ian Hibell and the Crane brothers as I first caught the cycling bug, and having the confidence to take my old steel-rimmed Raleigh to the Corsican mountains as a result.

Cameras, photography and diaries

It's nice to record your tour, but it's not worth messing up a good holiday with incessant, intrusive photo stops and endless posing. Your experience will live on in your head even if it's not on film.

This is not the place to offer a photographic primer, but a few pointers from someone who has seen altogether too many cycle tour photos:

» Pictures with people and bikes in are good! Pictures of bare roads and desolate landscapes can be good to set the mood, but it's nice to have some human interest too. If you're travelling alone, do all you can to get others to take pictures of you. Asking is a nice way to break the ice with a stranger, too.

» People looking at the camera is what you want. It's all too easy, when cycling as a couple, for one rider to take endless snaps of the other person's back. Instead, ride ahead and get the picture from the front: it makes a world of difference. It also helps if you can remove caps, helmets and the like so that you can see the person's face clearly.

» Try to fill the shot with what you're shooting – get up close!

» Try to get the sun behind the camera.

A great help in making photography quick and non-intrusive is to have your camera bag mounted on the handlebars, or in a handlebar bag. If you're not confident brandishing an expensive camera as you ride along, get a cheapie. Often, scenes you'd like to picture appear and are gone in an instant, and only if the camera is instantly to hand can you capture them.

Modern compact camera bags will provide adequate vibration protection when strapped straight to the bars. I usually add a releasable cable-tie as a backup to the bag's Velcro strap, but it's never been needed yet. My camera bag (a Lowe model) has a waterproof cover tucked away underneath which can be deployed in an instant, and the padding holds the camera firmly enough that I can leave it open in dry weather. So all have to do is pull the camera out, switch on, and shoot away – steering the bike with my spare hand!

What to ride

The vehicle you choose is, perhaps surprisingly, one of the less important aspects of touring, well behind the company you keep and the attitude you take. More or less anything that's reliable will get you there in the end – it's just a question of how much effort it'll take. There was one celebrated traveller who cycled across the USA on the notoriously flexible and fragile

Bickerton folder – if that's possible, anything is!

Of course, it's also irresistible for the technically-minded like myself to choose the most perfectly-optimised vehicle for touring, and so you'll see

cycle tourists using custom-made uprights, tandems with carefully-tuned braking systems, trailers for luggage, recumbents on two wheels and three, and not least, folding bikes. Your choice will depend on the nature of your tour, how much you need to use public transport, the size of your budget and garage, and the degree to which you enjoy attracting attention.

We've covered most of the main touring vehicle options in previous chapters. A few general thoughts, though. Get something with well-built wheels, as there's little more tedious than replacing drive-side spokes when away from your workshop tools. And unless you're supremely confident, take the loaded bike for a trial run before you set off.

Luggage

There are plenty of good panniers available, and now many manufacturers have 'completely waterproof' sealed plastic designs. Many are good, but the models from Ortlieb are still the 'gold standard'. On a recumbent, check out the likes of Radical, Arkel and Azub who make recumbent-specific bags shaped to make maximum use of your vehicle's luggage space.

These is another option, too: a trailer. Traditionally the advice has been wherever possible to keep the luggage on the bike; a single vehicle is easier to manhandle, keeps rolling resistance down and adds minimum weight. But loading up also puts a fair bit of stress on the bike frame, which needs to be built strong and heavy, and a heavy load in panniers can make bike handling problematic.

Trailers, on the other hand, can be attached even to relatively lightweight machines to add serious capacity without imposing too much strain on the frame. They're routinely employed on tandems, where it can hard to arrange enough luggage for a couple camping just in panniers.

Trailers can be awkward when the bike needs to be lifted or stored, but even that issue is addressed by trailers such as the Radical Cyclone and the Carry Freedom City – all fold or dismantle to some extent. See the chapter on load-carrying for details.

On the road

You'll swiftly develop a feel for touring, the habits and routines which make life easier. Check over the bikes each morning for any obvious problems, apply suncream well in advance, keep drinking, set an easy pace, keep an eye on the map for route-finding, and more.

There's actually quite a lot to think about and do, and that's one of the elements which makes cycle touring so relaxing. Travelling by bike involves you both physically and mentally, leaving little room for left-behind work worries or the like to intrude.

Give it a try!

Recumbents

Recumbent bikes – why?

Recumbent riding isn't for everybody – but every cyclist should give it a go! For some riders, some of the time at least, a recumbent can be a revelation. The comfort, the speed, the fun of zooming along close to the ground… it can make getting back on an upright seem strange after a while.

Comfort is the number one reason for recumbent riding. The full support of a seat rather than a narrow saddle combines with relaxed arms and wrists, plus a posture which doesn't require craning the neck to see in front. All that gets tired is your legs.

Speed may be a consideration for sporty types, but it's not usually the main motivation for going recumbent. Bikes with more extreme laid-back seating positions are certainly faster when you get up to speed or in headwinds, but most of the touring or city-type machines will be little if any faster than a normal bike. And on hills recumbents can often feel harder work, especially at first, as it can take several months for the

muscles to adapt to the riding position. In a mixed group recumbents will often fall behind on hills and catch up on the descent and on the flat – but it also depends on the rider.

Not being able to stand on the pedals, by the way, doesn't prevent recumbent riders from exerting just as much or more force: with the back braced against the seat you can push as hard as you like.

The safety situation

While we're on recumbent myths we have to touch on safety. The most frequently-expressed concern of potential recumbent riders is "I won't be seen – it's too low down", and most recumbent riders will be familiar with onlookers asking "Do you feel safe on that?". I was once passed, as I rode a recumbent, by a racing cyclist who darkly muttered "Tantamount to suicide, those things" as he went past!

Complete rubbish of course! Thousands of people ride recumbents, and while I couldn't back it up with statistics, I've never seen it suggested that the accident rate is worse than for upright bikes. In fact, all of the anecdotal evidence is that recumbents are noticed much more by motor vehicles, and you tend to get more respect and space on the road, not less.

You do need to take care when you may be obscured by walls or other vehicles, and many riders feel a flag makes you more visible in these situations. In town, it can be harder to see out at junctions, because you can't see over the traffic as you can with an upright. But behave like a vehicle and cycle well, and they're safe vehicles both in town and on the open road.

On the downside...

This lack of a good view in traffic applies in the countryside too: recumbent riders can miss out on views over walls and hedges. It can also be more awkward to converse with riding companions on upright bikes.

Other possible recumbent downsides include price – they're made in relatively small numbers, and there aren't many models that come in at under £1000 new. Second-hand can be a good way to dip a toe in the water.

Most cycle facilities are designed for diamond-frame uprights, and won't fit recumbents. So cycle spaces in trains, cycle parking lockers, and even cycle carriers for cars may well not fit – at least not without some adaptation. One answer is a folding recumbent, and we'll look at a few later.

There's also the undeniable fact that recumbents attract attention, and this can sometimes be unwelcome. Onlookers will ask questions, kids will shout comments, and you lose any chance at anonymity. But more positively, if you're in the right frame of mind then riding a recumbent can be a great way to break the ice and make friends.

Two or three wheels?

All of the above applies to recumbent trikes, too. Riders tend to divide into 'trike people' or 'bike people': I don't know many who regularly ride both. In favour of bikes is their simplicity, ease of storage, cost advantage – and the pleasure and dynamics of leaning through the bends. They're usually a bit faster and a fair bit lighter than trikes, too.

We'll discuss trikes in more detail later in this chapter. But if at all possible, do try both and see which you prefer…

Luggage and children

Many recumbents have carrier racks which accept normal panniers, and if available this is certainly the simplest solution. But only a few will accept four panniers, bringing them up towards the capacity of an upright tourer.

One solution is to use recumbent-specific luggage from the likes of Radical, AZUB or Arkel. These are panniers shaped to maximise the use of space behind and below a recumbent seat, with further capacity available in bags which fit snugly behind the seat back. Radical in particular make bags which simply slip over the seat of sportier, lower recumbents and hang down either side: this can be a good way to add touring capacity to a fast bike.

The other possibility is trailers. Both one-wheel and two-wheel trailers have their supporters. If you've already given up on taking your recumbent by public transport, the extra bulk of taking a trailer won't necessarily matter, and some will prefer the feel of towing a trailer to that of a fully-loaded bike.

Pulling a child trailer or Trets recumbent trailer bike is also, of course, very possible. I wouldn't recommend a childseat on any but the most upright of two-wheeled recumbents.

Researching

It's all too easy to over-research recumbents! You'll find opinion and info galore on the internet, and magazines too can be a distraction from what's important: actually trying them out! It really is a good idea to get some 'seat time' on a wide variety of bikes and trikes before looking into it too closely and developing pre-conceived notions of what might be right for you.

That said, there are several useful resources available:

» *Velo Vision* magazine, which has regular reviews of recumbent bikes and trikes. Tel 01904 438 224 or see www.velovision.com

» www.bentrideronline.com is a US-based online-only recumbent site, which does regular reviews of new bikes and also has a comprehensive Buyer's Guide, plus a very active forum.

» *Recumbent and Tandem Rider* is another US publication distributed free to dealers over there, but you can also subscribe via www.rtrmag.com. As the name suggests they do tests of both tandems and recumbents – in fact the mag mostly consists of road tests.

» *The Recumbent Bicycle* by Gunnar Fehlau is the only English-language book on the subject. Now in its second edition, it's available via dealers or the book trade, or see the publisher's website www.outyourbackdoor.com.

» The British Human Power Club has a regular newsletter. It tends to concentrate on racing, but also has technical features and event reports. They also publish *How to build an HPV*, a useful booklet for anyone thinking of building a recumbent from scratch. See www.bhpc.org.uk or call 01704 380 347 for more details.

Trying and buying

Dealers

Most bike shops don't stock recumbents: they take up a lot of space, they're hard to sell, and it's still a very limited market. That's good in a way, because it means that the recumbent industry can instead support a limited number of specialist recumbent dealers. A few other dealers may deal in one or two bikes, or source them to order, but are unlikely to stock them.

By going to a specialist you get good advice, the chance to actually try out the bikes (often on extended test-rides, or by hiring them for hours or days) and tuition to get you going. They're also great for backup should you need repairs, upgrades or specialist consumables like odd-sized tyres. Generally you'll need to make an appointment if you want to try bikes out: this allows the dealer to get them ready and set up for your height.

In the UK the main dealers are:

» Bikefix: London dealer with central location. Recumbent bike ranges from HP Velotechnik, Challenge and Burrows Engineering, also many trikes and uprights. Tel 020 7405 1218 or see www.bikefix.co.uk

» D-Tek HPVs: Dealer based in Ely, near Cambridge. Has a large stock of new and secondhand machines, and is a favourite with people who would like to try out many different machines at one visit (by appointment) and learn to ride recumbent. New bikes from HP Velotechnik and ICE amongst others, and also many cycle trailers. Rural setting is good for test rides. Tel 01353 648177 or email dtekhpvs@btconnect.com: no website.

» Futurecycles: East Sussex recumbent dealer with bikes from the Optima and Hase ranges, also specialising in learn-to-ride and day hire. They also sell trikes, uprights, folders and Moultons. Lovely rural location. Tel 01342 822847 or see www.futurecycles.co.uk

» Kinetics: Glasgow specialist in electric bikes, folders and recumbents. Sells the HP Velotechnik range, plus the low-racer from Toxy, the Tagun from Hase and bikes and trikes from Scooterbike. Tel 0141 942 2552 or see www.kbikes.com

» Laid Back Ligfiets: Enthusiast operation in Edinburgh offering recumbent learn-to-ride and tours, with links to the Ligfietswinkel recumbent shop in Amsterdam for sales. Challenge Mistral, Focus or Voss Bevo Bike available for hire. Also imports Nazca recumbents from the Netherlands.

Tel 07981 430159 or see www.ligfietswinkel.nl/Laidback.htm

» London Recumbents: Based in the capital's Dulwich Park. Hire and sales of Challenge and Hase bikes/trikes. Also do a lot of special needs cycling work. Tel 0208 299 6636 or see www.londonrecumbents.com

» Westcountry Recumbents (www.wrhpv.com, tel 0870 741 1227): Recently moved to Derby area despite the name. Trikes only, but included here as they also sell useful recumbent parts, tyres etc.

Events

Cycling events are a good place to meet the manufacturers and see the bikes. It can be hard, though, to get extended test rides, and often the circuits available are short and crowded. There are also often many interesting bikes brought along by visitors, and it may be possible to try these, too, if you ask nicely.

In the UK the annual York Cycle Show (Tel 0844 736 8456 or see www.yorkcycleshow.co.uk) in late June is probably the most worthwhile attending from a recumbent point of view. In recent years there have been more trikes than bikes on show.

Buying secondhand

Recumbents often come up second-hand, including classic older models like the Kingcycle pictured. Good places to look are:

» The *Velo Vision* website, where recumbents often come up on the free small ads: www.velovision.com. Also check out the small ads at www.bhpc.org.uk and www.cyclechat.co.uk, and on the CTC forum at www.ctc.org.uk

» D-Tek, if you prefer the reassurance of buying from a dealer.

» Small ads in the CTC magazine Cycle (see www.ctc.org.uk).

» Online at ebay.co.uk (caveat emptor, as always)

As with any other second-hand bike purchase, it's very much a gamble if buying sight unseen. If at all possible get a test ride first – if not, at least establish before you buy whether the bike will actually fit your leg-length!

The bikes

Here's a quick look at most of the recumbent bikes on the UK market today, sorted by type. After this section, we'll check out the trikes.

I've given approximate 'from' prices, but it's worth checking carefully which extras are included: adding carrier racks, mudguards etc can swiftly make a noticeable difference to the price.

Upright recumbents

Very easy to learn and ride – hop on and go! This format is also favoured for town riding and relaxed touring, as your head's relatively high. But while it's super-comfy and easy to get on with, this sort of bike can tend to feel a bit on the slow side for longer rides, and a more leaned-back position than these offer can be more comfortable over time – your weight isn't all on the buttocks, but spread over your back, too. But unless you spend hours at a stretch in the saddle, this may not matter, and you'll certainly enjoy the better view!

HP Velotechnik Spirit

Available from several of the UK dealers, this is a popular model. It has an aluminium main frame, and full suspension is standard. It adjusts to fit riders from around 5' to 6' 7", with a seat that slides easily along the frame. Accessories available include front fairing and

pannier racks. Prices start at £925 for an 8-speed derailleur version with V-Brakes.

Scooterbike

This is a more curvaceous design than the Spirit, with a somewhat lower bottom bracket, so if anything even more beginner-friendly. Like the Spirit, it has full suspension via a swingarm at the back and headtube

suspension at the front. Available in four different specifications via Kinetics, from £1145.

Optima Hopper

Nice-looking aluminium-framed upright recumbent from Optima, available with either dual-drive 3x9 transmission or the Shimano Nexus 7-speed hub gear. Rear suspension and luggage rack built in. Available from Futurecycles from around £1200.

Bacchetta Café

Long-wheelbase bike with relaxed riding position and easy beginner-

friendly ride. Long frame gives a noticeable suspension effect, and it's super-smooth. Useful quick-adjust for leg length means it fits a wide range of riders. Plenty of luggage options available for touring. From around £850 via dealers, or contact importers CycleCentric: tel +1 727 498 4600 or see www.cyclecentric. co.uk

Touring recumbents

Here's where I start to annoy manufacturers by missing out their bikes. Because touring and fast day riding is what recumbents do best, a huge number of models from around the world would qualify. I've limited it here to what's easily available in the UK, and will start with bikes ideal for loaded touring.

ICE B1

Launched in late 2008, the B1 is the first bike from the long-time trike builders ICE in Cornwall, UK, making it one of a very few UK-made recumbents. It's a well crafted and versatile bike, with a wide option list.

Key features include suspension, separating frame for transport, two handlebar designs and ICE's own wide-range derailleur gearing system. The ride is stable, smooth and touring-friendly.

Prices start at £1450, direct from ICE or via their dealers. See www.ice.hpv.co.uk or phone 01326 378 848.

Hase Tagun

Long-wheelbase design with adjustable-height suspension. Lovely relaxed ride and plenty of luggage capacity, plus limited folding. Easy to ride. Makes a fine

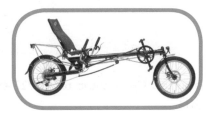

tourer with the optional rack and mudguards. Available from Hase dealers from around £1550.

HP Velotechnik Streetmachine, Grasshopper & Speedmachine Randonneur

A trio of machines from the respected German manufacturer. All now benefit from the 'Bodylink' hardshell seat which uniquely adjusts for length,

angle and degree of lumbar support. All are suspended, too. And all three have carrier racks available to fit a full touring load of four panniers, along with a vast range of well-developed accessories.

The Streetmachine is a real classic of the recumbent world, and it's been evolved for over a decade to result in the current 'GT version'. Well proven on tour and with solid frame and predictable handling it has few flaws. From around £1430 in the UK.

The Grasshopper fx has twin 20" wheels and an aluminium frame, making it noticeably more compact and

lighter than the Streetmachine. It has a slightly lower riding position, and a choice of above or below-seat steering. But the real stand-out feature is that the Grasshopper folds in half with the seat removed. The resulting package isn't tiny, but it will easily fit in most car boots. From around £1430.

The 'Randonneur' version of the Speedmachine brings this relatively low and sporty recumbent into this section. It's a little pricier (from around £1635) but offers mile-eating aerodynamics with plenty of comfort. They have several UK dealers, listed at the manufacturer website www.hpvelotechnik.com

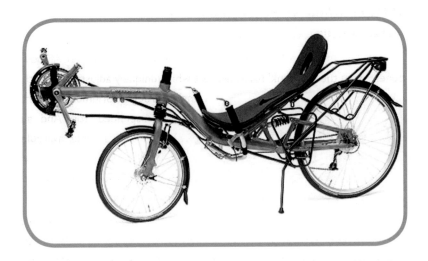

Challenge Hurricane, Mistral and Wizard

Deservedly popular as practical and good value tourers, the Challenge range from the Netherlands comprises more bikes than we can describe here. Perhaps the most popular in the UK have been the Hurricane and the slightly taller Mistral (from £1030) with 20" wheels all round, or the Wizard with a 26" rear wheel. The Hurricane and Mistral models really require recumbent-specific luggage or a trailer if you want to load up for a full tour, while the Wizard does have an extra rack available

The Challenge Seiran 24

for a second pair of panniers. There's now a slightly higher 'Tour' version of the Hurricane complete with front suspension, too, from £1190. All available from various dealers: see www.challengebikes.com

Optima Dragon, Orca & Condor

The Dutch are keen cycle tourists and Optima have catered for them for many years with high-seat short-wheelbase recumbents with good carrying capacity. The Dragon (from £1256) is perhaps the most approachable, with 20" front and 26" back wheel. The Orca and Condor both go for 26" wheels front and rear: this gives a lovely smooth ride over long tours and rough surfaces, easy tyre availability and a very stable, high position — but it can make starting, stopping and getting a foot down a little daunting for the less tall rider. The £1245 Condor is unusual in that the frame is stainless steel. The Orca is similar but in aluminium. All available via Futurecycles: www.futurecycles.co.uk. Manufacturer site is www.optima-cycles.nl

AZUB 4, Mini and MAX

The AZUB machines are competitively-priced (from around £1100) touring recumbents, mostly with full suspension, from the Czech Republic: UK buyers simply get the bike delivered to the door or via a dealer.

There's a full range, from twin-26"-wheeled off-road-oriented machines to the twin 20"-wheeled Mini, pictured, which has a high-tech look and a stable and solid ride. Their website www.azub.cz has full details, plus plenty of videos of the machines in action.

Fast touring and fun

Now for bikes which would be great for fast day-rides, light touring, or just messing around on. If you fancy, they could also be useful on the racetrack in one of the new 'practical' race categories offered by the British Human Power Club (www.bhpc.org.uk).

Burrows Ratcatcher

Fairly upright as recumbents go, and using the Burrows 'love it or hate it' scooped seat. Unique and stylish design, clever one-sided front suspension. Nine derailleur gears. Nice and light at around 12kg and comes with built-in tail fairing. Intended for fast day riding, audax and fun. Around £2000 from Burrows Engineering (01603 721 700) or Bikefix in London.

HP Velotechnik Speedmachine

With above-seat steering (two styles available) and free from the extra carrier racks of the Tour version, the fully suspended Speedmachine is fast and very comfortable – if not exceptionally light. From around £1795 from the various HP Velotechnik dealers.

Challenge Hurricane and SL models

The Challenge Hurricane (from about £1190) was a breakthrough model in its time, and spawned many imitations in the 'semi-low-racer' category. Low, fast and compact, it's been used for everything from racing to full-on touring. There's a 'Tour' version now with front suspension. Its one weakness has historically been its weight (around 15 kg) and that's been tackled with the sub 10 kg Hurricane SL (around £2200). This, and the other bikes in the 'SuperLight' series, are among the lightest production recumbents (barring real exotica!). Challenge have several UK dealers.

Optima Dolphin & Lynx

The Dolphin and Lynx (both from £1245) are practical, rear-suspension bikes with medium seat-height, and capable of carrying a fair bit of luggage. Neither are spectacularly light, but that's not what you're after on a tourer, anyway. With its longer wheelbase and 26" rear wheel the Lynx promises a more

stable, cushioned ride than the more nippy Dolphin – a prime case for a trip to Futurecycles for a test ride or two to decide your preference!

Nazca recumbents

Yet another manufacturer from the Netherlands (the world's largest

recumbent market), Nazca Ligfietsen (www.nazca-lig-fietsen.nl) make a well-developed range of bikes. I've ridden the Paseo, a very comfortable and ex-tremely stable mid-height fast tourer or fun bike, and was impressed. They have numerous other models

too. Imported by Laid Back Ligfiets in Edinburgh: 07981 430 159 or see www.laid-back-bikes.co.uk

Bacchetta recumbents

The sports bikes in the Bacchetta range from the USA take a different

approach from the various Netherlands machines, which seem to stress smooth curves as a key design element. The Bacchettas in contrast have a big bold and dead-straight main frame in oversized aluminium, and they're both light and fast. Models are available in various wheel size combinations and to suit your budget. If funds permit, do take a look at the £2700 Aero Titanium model, spectacularly light and with looks to match. Pictured here is the Corsa 24, a nicely-proportioned machine. Distributed in the UK via CycleCentric: Tel 01954 789284 or see www.cyclecentric.co.uk

Racing recumbents

If you're buying a recumbent for racing or all-out speed you probably don't need me to tell you what to get. But for inspiration, here's a speedy run-down of some of the models which may be suitable:

» Ratracer: the low fast one (pictured opposite) from Mike Burrows.

Contact Burrows Engineering (Tel 01603 721 700) or Bikefix.

» Toxy ZR: Clean design from Germany, available from Kinetics.

» M5, Challenge, Optima: all three of the Netherlands manufacturers produce exquisite, super-light race frames and bikes. If you're serious, get yourself over to Cycle Vision for a look.

» Velokraft: lovely carbon monocoque frames (pictured below) from Poland. Dealers in various countries but not the UK, so order direct from www.velokraft.com

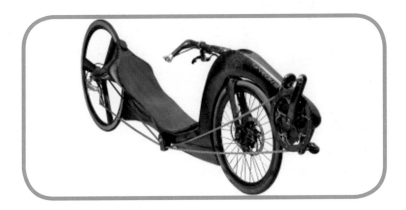

Trikes

Why a recumbent trike?

It's estimated – unscientifically – that recumbent trikes make up well over half of the recumbent sales in the UK. Why are they so popular?

Most obvious, perhaps, is the way in which they combine the comfort of a recumbent seat with the stability of a tricycle. Two-wheel recumbents aren't really difficult to ride, but the learning curve does put some people off, and even two-wheel fans would acknowledge that sometimes slow-speed handling can require concentration.

On a trike, however, you can go as slow as you like in complete relaxation, without balance problems and in a recumbent position that removes stress from back, wrists and neck. Many elderly or disabled cyclists find the recumbent trike gives back mobility and pleasure – and many modifications are possible. For example, you can control the machine via one arm only, or perhaps pedal with one leg – or use a hand-crank adaptation on some machines.

But a recumbent trike is also the first choice of many healthy, fit cyclists. There's certainly a fun-factor involved: riding a trike is just damn good fun. You're close to the ground for that additional feeling of speed, and braking and cornering on three wheels inspires confidence. Unlike on a two-wheeler, if you push the limits a bit and skid a wheel, it's no big deal – in most cases you'll just slide. And they're brilliant fun on snow and ice…

All of these factors make trikes ideal for touring, but they can also make great utility machines. Most offer good luggage capacity, and make excellent 'tractors' for trailer towing.

Of course, there are some downsides. Compared to two-wheelers they're relatively heavy, expensive and difficult to store and transport. Some people just prefer the feel of riding on two wheels. And as with many recumbents, they're low to the ground so you can't see over things – and many riders feel safer with a flag to advertise their presence. Usually, a trike is attention-catching enough to be very safe in traffic, but most fans would admit that congested city centres are not their ideal environment.

Types of trike

There are as many types of recumbent trike as there are of upright cycle. So you can buy a racing trike or a heavy-duty tourer; a child's model or a tandem. But most trikes follow now well-established layout and design principles – with a few interesting exceptions, of course!

The vast majority of recumbent trikes on the market today are 'tadpole' trikes: with two steered wheels in front and a single driven wheel at the back. This layout offers good handling and stability, especially in the 'worst case' of braking into a corner. Loosely speaking the rider's weight is thrown forward and between the two widely-spaced front wheels, so the trike won't tip. The drivetrain is simple, using essentially standard components except for a longer chain.

'Delta' trikes have the two wheels at the back, with the rider sitting between them for good cornering stability. The front wheel does the steering, and such bikes tend to be highly manoeuvrable. Most of the current models also let you link two or more such trikes together to form tandems or more – a bonus for couples whose pedalling power may not be evenly matched.

Suspension

A few years ago, suspension of any sort would be a rarity on a recumbent trike. But competition between the major brands and improving technology now means that rear suspension is widely deployed, and front suspension is now available if you want it.

It's arguable that for many riders suspension is a luxury, especially if you

mainly ride on smooth roads. A supportive seat and the long recumbent frame will take out much of the shock anyway. Nonetheless, rear suspension in particular comes with little weight or performance penalty these days, and it can smooth the ride noticeably, especially with narrow tyres. But don't rule a trike out if it doesn't have it

Relatively few trikes offer suspension on the front wheels, and it's only in the last year or so that a slew of full suspension models have appeared. This is largely driven by the popularity of velomobiles, streamlined trikes with a full body shell (see the end of this chapter). These require suspension as the rider can't so easily see the road surface, and because of the higher speeds they reach.

But for most riders, the additional complication is usually just not worth it. The impact of a front wheel hitting a bump is 'halved' at the centre of the

trike where the seat is mounted, so there's not such a huge benefit except on seriously bad road surfaces. There is inevitably a weight and cost penalty, too.

Luggage and accessories

Trikes typically carry luggage either side of the rear wheel, and touring models will often have specially-made carriers to accept up to four panniers – plus more on top. Most trikes also have rear dropouts standard enough to fit the hitches of commercially-available child or load trailers: check with the manufacturer if in doubt.

As to accessories, many items (lighting, for example) will be standard equipment, but some parts will have to be custom-made by the manufacturer. These include front mudguards (vital for UK conditions), mountings for mirrors and cycle computers, and possibly mountings for fairings.

Use of clipless pedals or similar to attach feet firmly to the pedals is strongly advised: if one slips off at speed and catches on the road, a nasty accident could ensue.

The trikes

Inspired Cycle Engineering

One of two UK-based trike manufacturers, Inspired Cycle Engineering in Cornwall are a long-established operation. Although in previous years they majored in custom-made trikes, recently the emphasis has been on their popular 'standard' models, the Q (for 'quick') and T (for 'touring'). The Q, pictured opposite, is rather lower-down and narrow, while the T is wider and more upright.

These models all come with rear suspension as standard, and there's a choice of mesh or solid-shell seats. They also either fold or disassemble very quickly for car boot transport, or can be taken down to even smaller pieces if necessary.

The list of accessories and possible upgrades is long, and the standard models can be equipped with racks, mudguards, mirrors, and more – they make fine touring machines as well as fun day-rides. Prices start at £1830.

Overall, I wouldn't hesitate recommending ICE trikes – I've ridden a fair few of them and they really are good. The manufacturers are keen, professional and ride what they build. They welcome visitors at their factory by appointment, and also sell via specialist dealers in the UK and worldwide. Contact them for details.

Tel 01326 378848 or see www.ice.hpv.co.uk

Greenspeed

Made in Australia, but with distribution in the UK and Europe, Greenspeed trikes are from another very long-established company – along with ICE and Windcheetah, among the original pioneers of commercial recumbent trikes.

Their trikes are divided between the GT and X series, produced to a standard spec, and their custom-built series of solo and tandem machines. These range from ultra-low racing trikes to the ultra-tough GTE expedition tourer, with its oversized pannier rack.

The GT models all fold in the middle (once the seat's removed), making them relatively straightforward to transport. New for 2008 is a low-maintenance hub-geared model. The X models are more oriented towards sporty riding, and like the GTs, come in a variety of specification levels. And all have a long list of options. Prices start at around £1900 in the UK.

Greenspeed also have a delta trike, the Anura (from £1975). With a differential system as standard to drive the two rear wheels, and an aluminium frame, it's a strong competitor to the Hase Kettwiesel. This layout is particularly easy to get on and off, thanks to the relatively high seat and easy access. A hitch kit to connect two Anuras together can be used to form a tandem (or more) 'chain'.

Finally, Greenspeed also make hand-cranked trikes and tandems, and are

one of the few manufacturers who are happy to sell parts and plans for homebuilders.

In the UK, Greenspeed models are sold via Westcountry Recumbents. See www.wrhpv.com or Tel 0870

740 1227. Greenspeed themselves are on Tel +61 3 9758 5541 or see www. greenspeed.com.au

Windcheetah

The Windcheetah is the trike that started the whole industry. From an original design by Mike Burrows, it's been evolved by Advanced Vehicle Design over many years.

It's still very much a Burrows design, with one-sided rear wheel support and aluminium tubes bonded into cast-aluminium lugs. They come together to make up a very light and stiff trike. It's quite narrow as trikes go, but the seat is nice and low, and the unique joystick steering almost encourages 'lean' to keep all three wheels on the ground.

A wide range of accessories, many beautifully-made in carbon fibre, have evolved over the years, including various luggage-carrying systems. And although many riders do use it for loaded touring, few would deny that the main thrust of the design is towards fast day-riding or even racing.

There are currently three models: top of the range is the £3970 Hypersport with carbon fibre all over. The Clubsport has a more standardised specification and comes in at around £2820. New for 2008 is the SportCompact, a tidy smaller version with 16" and 20" wheels, from £2585.

Tel 0161 928 5575 or see www.windcheetah.co.uk

Catrike: *Catrike Trail*

The Catrike range is imported from the USA, where this range of aluminium-framed trikes is one of the biggest sellers. They are good value

over here, too, with prices starting as low as £2000 if the importer has a special offer running! The trikes themselves come in seven different models from racing to touring. A popular choice is the

Trail, as pictured, which is a compact and lightweight machine. The 'direct' steering, with handlebars attached to the kingpins, isn't used on many other trikes, but it works well in practice.

Imported by WheelNV: Tel 0207 1937 085 or see www.wheelnv.co.uk. Manufacturer's website is www.catrike.com.

HP Velotechnik: *Scorpion fx and fs*

UPHP Velotechnik are one of Germany's largest makers of recumbent bikes, and the Scorpion was launched a few years ago as their first trike. It's a striking design with nicely styled frame and length-adjustable seat. Handling is smooth and predictable.

More recent models have added folding (remove the seat, and the main frame folds in half for a car-boot-sized package) and full suspension. This employs air shocks and an anti-roll bar, and is very neatly packaged.

The Scorpion models are available from a number of HP Velotechnik dealers in the UK, and prices start from around £2000, or £2600 for full suspension. Manufacturer's website is at www.hpvelotechnik.com

Challenge: *Trike*

Another trike from former two-wheel specialists, the Challenge trike is a clean design with a unique look and some clever engineering. The upward-sloping cross-beams give it a 'stance' very different from most bikes, and there are tidy details in the engineering of the kingpins, for example. As well as the rather lively direct-steer 'Concept' trike pictured, more calm-handling trikes with the usual

underseat steering bar are also available, as are heavy duty carrier racks for touring. From UK Challenge dealers from around £1700. See www. challengebikes.com for details and dealer list.

Anthrotech trike

A robust trike with high seat and wide track, with lovely plush rear

suspension. Has a reputation as a great utility trike – not for speed-merchants, but it carries loads really well on a wide rear carrier.

Prices: from £1790 via Bikefix, London. Tel 020 7405 1218 www.bikefix. co.uk. Manufacturer: see www.anthrotech.de

Hase: *Kettwiesel*

The Hase Kettwiesel successfully goes against the trend with its two-wheels at the back layout. This simplifies the steering no end, and the rider

is low enough between the rear wheels to make cornering great fun. You can also link two or more Kettwiesels to form a chain. Also, available with a vast range of adaptations for riders with disabilities. Single wheel drive models can struggle on steep hills or 'hop' the front wheel sideways under hard acceleration, but that's all cured by the optional differential system for two wheel drive.

Price: from around £1200.

Hase have several UK agents – contact them for details. Tel 0049 2309 782 582 or see www.hase-spezialraeder.de

KMX Karts: *Child and adult trikes*

The KMX trikes sprung out of a very different design approach: they're simply intended as great fun for kids! The super-affordable child's size trikes (currently starting at £234 inc VAT!) are robust and bombproof, as evidenced by plenty of stunt-riding footage on the KMX website. These are also great machines for kids with balance problem.

An adult range soon followed, and now KMX produce a range of five machines, with prices rising to £1750 for the top-of-the-range Venom pictured. There are both road and off-road (dirt riding) models included, plus a range of accessories. The seat has been much improved in recent machines, but as with all trikes, it's a good idea to try before you buy to check it suits your back.

Available via various dealers and distributors: contact KMX for details. Tel 023 92 750000 or see www.kmxkarts.com

Velomobiles

One particular class of recumbent trike deserves a special mention – the velomobile. With a full, streamlined body shell the rider is protected

from the weather, and the aerodynamic advantage is tremendous. Research in the Netherlands concluded that riding at 30 km/h (around 20 mph) an upright bike rider might have to put out 250W – quite hard work, even for an athletic rider. In a Quest velomobile (as pictured above) it would take just 100W – a pace which a fit rider can keep up for hours.

Speeds and distances which would be impossible on a normal bike or trike become feasible year-round – and if you're not convinced, most models also offer the option of electric assist.

The downsides, as so often with interesting bikes, are weight and cost. The weight penalty isn't necessarily such a big deal, in most terrain at least, and the extra speed both downhill and on the flat more than compensates in most cases. Another issue may be the space required for parking – secure ideally, as the fairings can be easily damaged. And riders had better not be shy!

Other velomobile benefits include tremendous road presence and safety: the bodyshell protects the rider in a crash. There's usually waterproof luggage space, and the drivetrain is also often enclosed for low maintenance.

There are now numerous manufacturers around the world, and in 2008 alone several new models were launched, including machines from established trike makers ICE (pictured) and Greenspeed. I really can't do the subject or the various models justice in the space available here, so must refer readers to the internet – just search on 'Velomobile'.

With prices usually in the £3000+ range, a velomobile is a significant investment, but it can offer human-powered performance unlike any other sort of bike or trike. Is this the ultimate in pedal-powered transport?

Further reading

Magazines

Velo Vision: the quarterly magazine edited and published by the author of this book. Includes regular reviews of transport and specialist cycle designs, cycle culture and brings you specialist supplier advertising. Sample copies and subscriptions are available direct from the publisher (Tel 01904 438 224, www.velovision.com) and via a few selected dealers – not (yet) on the newsstands! There's also a full digital edition and free sample issue online: see the website. Full colour, around A4.

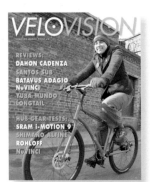

A to B: Long-running magazine specialising in folding and electric bikes, as well as wider UK transport matters (trains etc). Very thorough reviews and the best place to go for electric bike information in particular. They cover other practical cycling (family, load-carrying) on and off, too. A5, full colour. Tel 01305 259 998 or www. atob.org.uk

Bicycle Quarterly: Scholarly publication from the USA principally covering lightweight 'randonneur' cycles, but with truly excellent technical investigations relevant to just about all cyclists. A4ish, mono. See www.bicyclequarterly.com

Practical Pedal: Oregon, USA-based publication giving a voice to the nascent practical cycling movement in the USA. Issues available on paper and also as a free download from their website: www.practicalpedal.com

Momentum: A fresh and stylish free-circulation magazine from Vancouver, Canada, with plenty of features relevant outside their region. Again, get the PDF free from their website: www.momentumplanet.com

Books

City Cycling: Richard Ballantine, author of the classic 'Richard's Bicycle Book' is back with a new guide for a new generation of cyclists. The book to buy if you want sensible, clear advice on starting out with bikes, and more detailed advice on traffic cycling techniques. ISBN 978 1905 005604, www. snowbooks.com

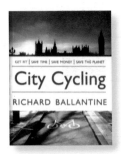

Bicycle Design: Mike Burrows explains what

really matters when you design a bike, working from basic principles and minus the marketing hype. Great reading for practical pedallers who want their bikes to really work, not just look good.   ISBN 978 1905 005680, www.snowbooks.com

Cyclecraft: John Franklin's recently updated and still definitive guide to advanced cycling techniques. An empowering book for those who feel shaky in traffic: the techniques really work and give you control of you own safety. ISBN 978 011 7037403, www.cyclecraft.co.uk

Cycling for profit: Jim Gregory of Bikes at Work in the

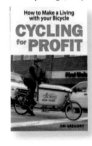

USA offers advice for anyone looking to make money through cycling: cycle courier and pedicab services are emphasised, but he has other ideas as well! Essential reading for anyone starting out in a bicycle business (or perhaps just dreaming of doing so...) www.bikesatwork.com

Bicycling Science by David Gordon Wilson: Definitive, academic in tone but fascinating for all who want to delve into the first-principles, basic science behind cycling – and which underpins all practical cycling design. 500+ pages, around A5. ISBN 0-262-73154-1, MIT Press.

Websites

» velovision.com: Regular updates from the practical and specialised cycle industry and community. Free small ads, forum, magazine index and more.

» bentrideronline.com: US-based recumbent cycling resource, with reviews and more. The BROL forum is probably the most popular English-language forum for recumbent riders.

» foldsoc.org.uk: Folding Society website, with folding bike news and detailed pages on particular models.

» citycycling.co.uk: online monthly magazine with a fresh take on UK urban cycling: distinctly more arts, culture and social commentary than anything technical.

» cyclechat.co.uk: perhaps the most friendly of the large UK cycling forums. Sub-sections cover commuting, specialised bikes, touring and cake-stopping!

» bhpc.org.uk: the British Human Power Club. Of interest not just to those planning on racing recumbents, but also for anyone interested in building a bike: there's a helpful forum and a 'how-to' booklet too.

» tandem-club.org.uk: Useful resource for those getting into tandeming, with a discussion forum where questions will be answered by experienced tandemists.

» ctc.org.uk: The UK national cycle organisation has a sprawling website, but it's especially worth seeking out the technical pages which contain much useful advice. Join up to support their lobbying work and also for benefits including free legal aid and third party insurance.

» www.sheldonbrown.com: a definitive technical site, but also rich in riding wisdom. Sheldon (sadly deceased in early 2008) explains even technical arcana with beautiful simplicity and impeccable accuracy.

» crazyguyonabike.com: a site where cycle tourists can conveniently place tour reports, updating from 'on the road'. A busy site where any potential cycle tourist can find advice, information and inspiration.